Spiritual Warfare

Our Weapons Are Not of This World

Other books by Rick Upchurch

Discipleship with James

A Guidebook for Curriculum Development and Assessment

Spiritual Warfare

Our Weapons Are Not of This World

Rick Upchurch

Tools to Lead Publishing

Spiritual Warfare:

Our Weapons Are Not of This World

Published by Tools to Lead Publishing
www.toolstolead.com

Printed in the United States of America

All biblical quotes are from the New International Version, © 1973, 1978, 1984 by International Bible Society

ISBN: 978-0-9833239-3-8

I am dedicating this book to my parents, Clay and Opal Upchurch. I had the privilege of being raised in a godly home, by godly parents who took seriously their responsibility to raise their children with morals and ethics.

My parents lived out a sincere faith which impacted my life and all who know them. Because of their example I have discovered my own personal faith in Jesus Christ. I can only pray that I do as much for my own children.

Rick Upchurch

TABLE OF CONTENTS

PREFACE

I am not sure when I first noticed it, but there was no doubt in my mind as I stood to preach that Sunday night what had been happening. We had just prayed over a cloth anointed with oil for the healing of one of the body of believers where I served as pastor, and a young lady stood to sing; as she sang her praises to God, I felt His spirit wash over me in a powerful way. I sat there, practically overwhelmed with a sense of the Spirit and power. In those moments, God revealed to me what I had seen, but not understood. In the preceding months I had begun to teach a series of lessons on spiritual warfare. About that time things began to happen in the congregation: deaths, sickness, personal trauma, financial disasters. You would think I would have made the connection; after all, these are merely the manifestations of warfare in a higher realm. Within a few weeks, however, even though the negative effects of the battle were still being felt, God's power began to break through into the life of the congregation. Four individuals over the course of two weeks, individuals with little or no contact with the church, were saved. The previous Sunday, six people came forward to be sanctified, baptized by the Holy Spirit. Worship, an important part of what goes on at our church, became endued with a special power, even though those leading were untrained and developing their own style. As I stood to preach, God redirected my message to unity in the battle and perseverance.

Over the next few months and years God has shown me some aspects of the battle and how to be effective as a spiritual warrior. This book is about those strategies, tactics, and weapons. I believe in the final victory but I also want to be as effective for the Lord as possible on a day-to-day basis. The lessons contained in the following pages will give you a different way of looking at life, and, I hope, new tools to be victorious in your own personal battle.

I would like to express my appreciation for the interest and assistance of Jennifer Epperhart, who deciphered my handwriting to type the rough draft. Her enthusiasm helped keep things going when I was tempted to procrastinate. I also want to express my appreciation to Chris Matzinger who encouraged me greatly as I was developing this material and was helpful in proofreading the early manuscripts. Rev. David Amstutz and Mike Northcutt also spent a great deal of time reading through the manuscript, asking some hard questions, and making valuable suggestions.

I want to thank my wife Mary Margaret, whose faith and belief in me has never wavered. Her life in the face of great trials has proven the principles contained within these pages. Her constant testimony of God's great love has been an inspiration to all who know her. She provided great help in preparing the final version of this book.

CHAPTER 1
INTRODUCTION: THE BATTLEGROUND

> With the secularization of our worldview, the reality of spiritual warfare has almost disappeared from our thinking; and rather than risk the scorn of our peers, we seek to have as little to do with the world of demons as possible, being content to leave them in the realm of theory or theology. To bring them into everyday life would be to risk ridicule; and that is something none of us likes and very few of us handle well.[1]

The entire concept of spiritual warfare is one which polarizes the Christian community. Discussions of demons and demonic strongholds in lives is laughed at by many Christians as, perhaps, possible on the mission fields, but certainly not in an enlightened and civilized society. For such individuals, the thought of spiritual warfare is nonsense, yet these same people struggle in their Christian lives to maintain focus and overcome temptation. Their lives lack any semblance of the power or victory described in the New Testament, except in momentary flashes, and then usually only at public worship.

The demonic forces of this world prey upon such ignorance in their continuous battle to steal glory from God by damning the creatures which were created in His likeness for His fellowship. Their work is vastly simplified when the church discounts or ignores their reality.

---

[1]Timothy M. Warner. *Spiritual Warfare, Victory over the Powers of this Dark World* (Wheaton, IL. Crossway Books, 1991), 59.

The work of demons is primarily focused in two distinct areas:

Maintenance

Demonic activity is primarily directed at maintaining an atmosphere where Christianity is largely ignored and/or ridiculed by the majority of the population. I call this the "prison mode." The task at which these demons work is to make sure that no positive information about God, Jesus, or salvation ever reaches anyone who is not already a Christian. They use the media to make Christians and religion seem phony or irrelevant. Every effort is made to keep the truth about salvation from the ears of a non-believer. Unfortunately many who profess the name of Christ add to Satan's efforts at maintenance. For example, whenever those who profess Christ continue in a lifestyle of sin, those already in the prison mode conclude that a relationship with Jesus is a meaningless addition to life. This might be likened to "friendly fire" in which a soldier targeting the enemy accidently hits his comrades. Satan has effectively uses "friendly fire" to further his own war against heaven and is example of that how we live our lives does make a difference for those around us.

Let's look at some other examples. A television sitcom portrays a Christian as dogmatic and legalistic, concerned only about the law and with no concern for mercy or grace. This portrayal makes it seem as if all Christians are legalists who experience none of the joy of God's presence, only the bindings of "Thou shalt not." Another example is the portrayal of the Christian who twists their faith and uses it as an excuse for behavior which is purely selfish. Even non-Christians recognize this as hypocrisy and insist that the church is filled with either the legalist or the hypocrite. Thus, Satan's lies work well in keeping many in the prison mode. There *are* legalists and hypocrites in the church. We often forget that the church is the *best* place for sinners of all kinds to come and find true faith, including the legalists and hypocrites. Unfortunately, while they are the minority, too often their actions speak louder than do the words and actions of the faithful.

Attack

The second area of demonic activity is the seduction of those who have claimed a relationship with Christ that takes them away from their faith, and back into the chains of sin. The material in this book largely addresses this second emphasis of demonic activity. As you will see throughout this book, demons have many tactics and strategies which have consistently proven effective against the unwary.

As the former pastor of a holiness church, I became increasingly concerned over the dearth of material which actually deals with the principles of spiritual warfare from the basis of the holiness tradition. In talking with fellow pastors about my study on spiritual warfare, their response indicates unfamiliarity with the subject. Although a part of that unfamiliarity may be due to terminology, another part is reflective of Warner's statement quoted at the first of this chapter. We do not want to believe in demons and demonic activity! We refuse to talk about demons and even think about their reality, hoping that they will take the hint and go away. Unfortunately, they do not.

Sanctification, explained more fully later, is powerful in bringing victory to the believer, but because we have lost sight of the battle, much, if not most, of the effectiveness of the sanctified life is wasted and many succumb to the battle, not because they are incapable of the fight, *but because they are ignorant of the attack*. Without a strong relationship founded upon a deep faith, when the attacks come it is only a short time until frustration and despair, and even false guilt, set in. When this happens the believer either retreats into a stagnant state or simply gives up and falls back into the "prison mode." The battle is ongoing. To lose sight of that reality is to fall into Satan's plans for our own destruction.

One weakness of the holiness movement has been to assume that once the concept of sanctification is understood, one need not be concerned about the individual anymore, that sanctification automatically results in maturity is *practically* accepted even though *intellectually* denied. To be fair, this is never suggested or promoted by holiness literature. In fact, quite the opposite is emphasized again and again. Ralph Earle, one of the great scholars of the holiness movement in the Church of the Nazarene, writes of Luke 22: 42 ("Father, if you are willing, take this cup from me; yet not my will, but yours be done."), "So the verse may be taken as indicating two crises--a crucial conversion and a complete consecration--and *then a continual following Christ the rest of our lives.*"[2] (Italics added). The emphasis

---

[2]Ralph Earle, *Sanctification in the New Testament* (Kansas City: Beacon Hill Press, 1988), 15.

here is upon the continual following. It is regrettable that many who have experienced the infilling of the Holy Spirit have lost that presence due to a lack of attention to the disciplines which lead to spiritual maturity.

There can be no doubt that such a battle is being waged. Daniel 10:12-14 reveals a glimpse of that battle when the angel sent with a message from God declares:

> Since the first day that you set your mind to gain understanding and to humble yourself before your God, your words were heard, and I have come in response to them. But the prince of the Persian kingdom resisted me twenty-one days. Then Michael, one of the chief princes, came to help me, because I was detained there with the king of Persia. (Dan. 10:12-13)

The prince of the Persian kingdom indicates a "geographical" demon, that is, one who is in charge of a geographic region. It required Archangel Michael's intervention for the message to get through.

Paul uses many different analogies to describe the steps to success in the Christian life, none more powerful than his reference to the armor of God and spiritual warfare. In 2 Corinthians 10:3-4, Paul continues a militaristic theme with an important difference; the weapons of spiritual warfare, he says, are not the weapons of physical warfare. This is an important distinction for those who are sincere in the battle. *Any action which seeks its solutions with the wrong weapons has an uncertain future.* This is especially true in spiritual warfare. A case in point would be the physical attacks on abortion clinics and the doctors who perform abortions. While it is desirable from a spiritual point of view to halt this detestable practice, to use physical weapons to that end not only is largely unsuccessful, but throws those who use such weapons into the same situation as Saul, the first king of Israel, when he tried to do things his way and so lost his kingdom and blessing (1 Samuel 13). When we use the weapons of this world without first dealing appropriately with the problem in the spiritual world, our success and even our spiritual life is in danger.

As to the actual battleground of spiritual warfare, Ephesians 6:12 highlights that quite well:

> For our struggle is not against flesh and blood, but against the rulers, against the authorities, against the powers of this dark world and against the spiritual forces of evil in the heavenly realms.

The reference to the battleground being in the heavenly realms is a bit unclear to us earth-bound mortals. Add to this the reference found in Daniel and one is given the impression that there is more going on around us than meets the eye.

Perhaps the best way to describe the perceived difference in the physical world and the spiritual realm would be to refer to the six blind men who first came into contact with an elephant. The first one, feeling the trunk declared the elephant to be like a snake. The second, feeling the leg, proclaimed the elephant to be in reality like a tree, the third one, touching the large ears, knew the elephant was like a fan, and the fourth feeling the tail imagined the elephant was much like a rope. Just so it is in discussing the reality we know. We, who are in contact with reality, see what we see and know what we know and there is no doubt that this is reality. However, God's view of the world is quite different. He sees the big picture. So we are left with coping with our perceived reality with the knowledge *it is only part of the picture.* Herein enters faith; faith in God and faith that He sees the big picture and really will do as He says in His word and take care of us. It is like a huge tapestry. We are the thread which from one view is chaotic and from another is organized; from one view confusing and from another clear. God weaves the threads of our lives into the tapestry, and we trust Him to do so. Yet He will only work with the lives of those who choose to be used. Spiritual disciplines, if you will allow the comparison, make the threads of our lives strong and vibrant for God's design.

From the divine perspective the battleground of the heavenlies is not only "real," but more pertinent to those of us who walk this earth than is obvious to the eye. Yet, to engage in warfare on this battleground, as did Daniel, requires that we first gain victory on another battleground. That battleground is the battleground of the heart and it is here where most get stuck. This battleground is where we first become aware of our need for salvation. It is where we deal with guilt and "wrestle" with sin's effects. It is where the carnal nature is exposed and dealt with. It is where demonic strongholds are revealed and demolished. The battle for an individual's heart is of prime importance both to God and Satan, but it is largely one that is fought by us, with ourselves. God provides the weapons, the presence of his Spirit and the strength to go into battle. However, Satan's demons and our own carnal nature will also be there to lie, deny, and attempt to thwart any progress that is made. The battle for the heart has left many causalities, as well as Christians "saved, sanctified, and petrified," unable to exist on meat and provide a spiritually mature base for service or growth, a kind of spiritual stagnation. Mario Murillo calls

such individuals "high maintenance/low impact converts."

> Because of them, pastors dare not preach past noon. They are the reason leaders burn out. These preemies demand constant care and yield nothing in the way of service. In many charismatic churches, leaders are neglecting prayer, evangelism, and vision as they blindly try to counsel entertain, and lend life support to this group that never seems to grow out of danger.... Since they are born with an inflated sense of self-importance, they interpret every scripture and define every experience from a 'what can it do for me' attitude.

> As they boast of great authority, they crumble at the first wave of adversity. They know of all their biblical rights but none of their responsibilities.

> Their common bond is that they are users, not givers. Their fickleness has leaders in a panic, running to keep them distracted. These brats call pastors at all hours for even trivial problems until the leader collapses.

> They have no thirst for depth, no long-term commitment, no faith beyond feeling, and no sense of mission to a hurting world. The thought of denying self to grow and be equipped to touch other is like quantum physics to them.[3]

This book deals extensively with the battleground of the heart and

the principles, strategies, and tactics necessary to be victorious. Each

chapter presents a different aspect of the battle and gives "hands on" tools

for overcoming the enemy's attacks. We will look at the real power

available to Christians, how to access that power, and apply it for the glory

of God. Although spiritual warfare is becoming a popular theme, this

battleground is almost totally ignored in our day. Because of this, I believe,

Christianity is often portrayed as weak and insipid. Nothing could be

---

[3]Mario Murillo, *Fresh Fire* (Anthony Douglas Publishing, Danville, CA 1991), 15-17.

further from the truth. Until you have achieved victory in the battleground of the heart, you will be frustrated and defeated in achieving much of the results possible to the fully trained warrior.

Spiritual Warfare, is a discipleship manual. It seeks to take you to a new awareness of God's plan for your life and give you the tools necessary to accomplish that plan. It can be used individually or in small groups. The principles in the following pages should generate some interesting discussions in a group setting as well as prompt some deeper questions for the individual seeking his way to a deeper walk with Christ.

Questions:

1. How would you interpret Ephesians 6:12? Is there really a battle going on?

2. Does the thought of wrestling against the forces of Satan affect your commitment to the cause of Christ? Why or why not? How would you interpret "wrestling" with the dark forces of this world?

3. In what areas of your personal life can you most clearly see the battle? What area of your life gives you the greatest difficulty in overcoming spiritually?

4. Read 1 Samuel 13. Saul's behavior seems understandable from our perspective but is condemned. What messages did he tell himself he was sending and what messages did God understand from his actions? Examine your life and the messages your actions send. Do you ever fall prey to Saul's mindset?

5. How does 2 Corinthians 10:3-4 address Saul's and our situations?

CHAPTER 2
FIRST THINGS FIRST

The initial point of contact in this struggle for the heart comes when the Holy Spirit, through one agency or another, makes an individual aware there is a better way to live now, and hope for eternity. The Holy Spirit's influence might come from a sermon, Sunday school teacher, television, radio, the beauty of a sunset, the splendor of the night sky, the loving word of a friend, the harsh word of an opponent, the faithful lifestyle of a friend, etc. Whatever the source, now the individual is aware that there is another style of life, one which promises the presence of unconditional forgiveness, love, and eternal life. It is impossible to fully describe this moment; it truly has to be experienced to understand the impact and words cannot do it justice.

Before this realization there was no battle. Satan clearly had full control, even if the individual had lived a relatively pure life. In fact, the individual was probably unaware of Satan's ownership of his soul. As long as Christ was kept out of the picture, the individual was trapped in a spiraling downward destiny. Scripture draws aside the curtain to reveal the truth Satan would prefer to conceal:

Romans 3:23 "for all have sinned and fall short of the glory of God."

Romans 6:23 "For the wages of sin is death, but the gift of God is eternal life in Christ Jesus our Lord.'

Now, however, there is a choice to be made, and depending on the choice, a battleground to enter:

a) Reject this new truth and continue to live as before, or

b) Believe the Holy Spirit's influence and accept Jesus Christ's love and forgiveness.

This battle may last only minutes from the point of realization that there is a new way of life, to years. There are several factors which contribute to the length of this battle. One of those is called the Readiness Principle. The Readiness Principle says that there is a point or points in a person's life when they are more likely than at other points to consider accepting Jesus Christ as Lord. Simply put, each person has a Readiness Quotient (RQ), which varies as the circumstances around us vary. As trauma increases, the RQ generally increases to a level where acceptance of Christ is perceived as a viable option. When trauma is low or non-existent, the RQ is correspondingly low and the acceptance of Christ as Lord is discounted as a viable option. A low RQ indicates that things seem to be going well and why should a life change even be considered? A high RQ would be associated with such circumstances as: marriage, death, birth of a child, loss of a job, divorce, major illness, or other major life changes. One of the roles of the Holy Spirit is to bring an awareness of our need of God into our lives at just the right time so that we might give serious consideration to Christ, this is called "conviction." When we experience crisis, especially those with a high RQ, the Holy Spirit often brings a godly witness into the picture whose life or testimony will open the door for the message of Christ to be considered. Those who have not accepted Christ as

Lord are tuned to the reality of this world and less likely to see the peril hanging over them as they continue in the prison mode. The combination of RQ and the work of the Holy Spirit opens the eyes of these captives to the truth which Satan had been hiding: *that Jesus' love is without measure and his forgiveness for our sins, full and free.*

Scripture is the window into this new lifestyle. The Bible, inspired by God sets forth the reality of a new way of life for anyone, regardless of race, sex or intelligence. In God's word, there are clear references to the "non-saved," pre-acceptance of Christ state I've labeled the prison mode.

> Proverbs 4:19 - "But the way of the wicked is like deep darkness; they do not know what makes them stumble."

> Luke 1:79 – "to shine on those living in darkness and in the shadow of death, to guide our feet into the path of peace."

> Luke 11:34 - "Your eye is the lamp of your body. When your eyes are good, your whole body also is full of light. But when they are bad your body also is full of darkness."

> Ephesians 5:11 - "Have nothing to do with fruitless deeds of darkness, but rather expose them."

> Ephesians 6:12 - "For our struggle is not against the authorities, against the powers of this dark world and against the spiritual forces of evil in the heavenly realms."

> Colossians 1:13 - "For he has rescued us from the dominion of darkness and brought us into the kingdom of the Son he loves."

> 1 Peter 2:9 - "But you are a chosen people, a royal priesthood, a holy nation, a people belonging to God, that you may declare the praises of him who called you out of darkness into his wonderful life."

> 2 Peter 2:4 - "For if God did not spare angels when they sinned, but sent them to hell, putting them into gloomy dungeons to be held for judgment;"

Jude 1:6 - "And the angels who did not keep their positions of authority but abandoned their own home--these he has kept in darkness, bound with everlasting chains for judgment on the great day."

Clearly, the individual who does not know Jesus Christ personally as Savior and Lord of his life not only must deal with trauma and life without the assurance of God's love, but faces a bleak future of eternal damnation.

Once the individual becomes aware of the opportunity of salvation, the battle has begun. Now Satan must combat these truths with every measure at his disposal. Through a mixture of lies, deceptions, physical pain, broken relationships, and temptations he will attempt to regain full control and shut out any godly influence. Here again the work of the Holy Spirit is going on even when we are unaware of the battle taking place. The Holy Spirit continues to draw the individual into the awareness of God's love until truth blossoms and are no longer satisfied with the lifestyle of sin. They are ready to be made into new creations, set free from the bondage of sin. 2 Corinthians 5:17 declares, "Therefore, if anyone is in Christ, he is a new creation; the old has gone, the new has come."

Jesus' sacrifice was for the specific purpose of providing a new destiny for our souls and a new way of living right now. The path to this new beginning is short and simple: confession of Jesus as Lord, repentance of our sin, and belief in Jesus' ability to forgive. Confessing Jesus to be the Lord of our life can be a big step. It is acknowledging that on our own we are helpless to live rightly. Jesus' love is the answer for our dilemma and as we confess him as Lord the next step is to repent of our sin. Sin can be defined in a variety of ways but the easiest way to understand it is that sin is that which violates the known law of God. God and sin don't mix. Once we become aware that sin not only separates us from God, denying us access to his love, but that it literally hurts God, we are ready to repent of those sins. Repentance is the genuine sorrow for committing the sin and a turning away from it. The final piece is the belief that Jesus is able to forgive us our sins and still love us.

> Romans 10:9 "That if you confess with your mouth, "Jesus is Lord," and believe in your heart that God raised him from the dead, you will be saved."

> Romans 10:10 "For it is with your heart that you believe and are justified, and it is with your mouth that you confess and are saved."

> l John 1:9 "If we confess our sins, he is faithful and just and will forgive us our sins and purify us from all unrighteousness."

> Luke 13:3 I tell you, no! But unless you repent, you too will all perish.

> Luke 15:7 I tell you that in the same way there will be more rejoicing in heaven over one sinner who repents than over ninety-nine righteous persons who do not need to repent.

> Acts 3:19 Repent, then, and turn to God, so that your sins may be wiped out, that times of refreshing may come from the Lord,

> Acts 17:30 In the past God overlooked such ignorance, but now he commands all people everywhere to repent.

> 2 Corinthians 7:10 Godly sorrow brings repentance that leads to salvation and leaves no re ret, but worldly sorrow brim s death.

Many feel unworthy of this great salvation, but in fact, we all are unworthy, yet He loves us anyway. It is not because we are worthy, but because of His love that salvation is possible. Our feelings of unworthiness are turned against us by the liar, Satan, to make us stop short of receiving salvation. For others, the seeming easiness of confession, repentance, and belief sounds too good to be true. Some are more than willing to *buy* their salvation, or do whatever it takes to *make* it happen, but to simply confess and believe sounds too easy. Indeed, this is one of the enemy's favorite ploys. If Satan can convince the individual that a certain level of "goodness" must be achieved before salvation can be attained, he can delay the release from his prison of lies until it become a prison of eternal damnation. It is NOT by works that we are saved, but by FAITH (Ephesians 2:9). There is no salvation apart from belief. It is this which makes us equal before the Lord.

There is no way to adequately explain the sensation that comes at the moment of salvation. For many there is a strong emotional release compiled with great joy, for others there are tears and a sense of quiet peace. In some the feeling is one of victory, in others there is a sense of a freedom from guilt. Some experience no "feeling" at all, others report a sense of being forgiven, while others talk of the overwhelming presence of pure LOVE. Yet, in spite of the variety of emotional effects, or lack of them, this moment is the beginning of a new chapter in the life of the believer; before he was lost and doomed, now he has been adopted as a child of God and given an inheritance of eternal life.

It is crucial right at the onset of spiritual warfare to keep in mind that Satan is a liar and that salvation is by faith. As long as we believe, *regardless of how we feel,* salvation is ours. Feelings are transitory things which are affected by the circumstances of our lives. Often Satan uses the lack of specific feelings to declare that, "nothing has happened," and, "you cannot possibly be saved because you don't 'feel' saved." This mixture of truth with lie (true we don't "feel" saved, but remember salvation is by faith, *not feelings)* is often successful in deceiving the new Christian into giving up his faith and falling into even deeper despair about being able to become a Christian at all. *The Holy Spirit will make us aware of the change in natures somehow,* but we will not always "feel" it. It is imperative that the new warrior begin a daily practice in the use of the spiritual weapons described later in this book.

If you do not have the assurance that Christ is your Savior, then why not stop here and repeat this prayer below aloud as a sincere, repentant, expression of your heart.

> *Dear Jesus, I know that I have sinned and am separated from You. I know You love me and died so that I might be saved. I confess my sinful life is wrong and I turn from that life and accept Your forgiveness and love. Amen.*

Questions

1. List ways by which Satan keeps the unsaved person from either hearing the gospel message or taking it seriously.

2. How did the message first intrude upon your consciousness? What was your response.

3. Studies have indicated that it takes from 7 to 12 exposures to the gospel before salvation is accepted. Did you go through a period of rejecting or denying the gospel before you received? What was your reasoning?

4. Describe how confession and repentance work hand in hand?

5. Did you have a specific "feeling" when you accepted Christ? Describe that feeling.

6. How much a part of your relationship with Christ is dependant upon keeping that same feeling in place? Why is this a dangerous game?

7. In what way is "salvation by faith alone" the great equalizer?

CHAPTER 3
SANCTIFY THEM...

"...the task of the church is not to make men and women happy; it is to make them holy."[4] (Charles Colson)

Satan fears virtue. He is terrified of humility; he hates it. He sees a humble person and it sends chills down his back. His hair stands up when Christians kneel down, for humility is the surrender of the soul to God. The Devil trembles before the meek, because in the very areas where he once had access, there stands the Lord, and Satan is terrified of Jesus Christ.[5] (Francis Frangipane)

The emphasis Frangipane has upon humility is a "back door" approach to the theme which is foundational to holiness churches, namely: before we can be victorious in the battle we must submit fully to the commander, God, and yield ourselves totally to His orders. In other words, we must be sanctified. In 1 Thessalonians 4:3 Paul declares, "It is God's will that you should be sanctified"

1 John 1:5 pictures God as light and Christians are admonished to walk in the light (v.7). As has already been described, Satan's forces are equated with darkness and any darkness intentionally harbored in the soul provides a seedbed for our destruction. An illustration might be likened to a surgery for the removal of a cancer; extra tissue around the cancer is also

---

[4] Charles Colson, *The Body: Being Light in the Darkness* (Word Publishing, 1992), 46.

[5] Francis Frangipane, *The Three Battlegrounds* (River of Life Ministries, Cedar Rapids, IA, 1989), 9.

removed in an attempt to get every single cell of the cancer. To leave even one cell behind means that it will grow and spread again.

C.W Ruth in the classic, *Entire Sanctification Explained*, gives three steps to achieving just such an operation that will bring us into a state of holiness where light prevails. "**First**, there should be the positive assurance, or witness of the Spirit to a present acceptance with God."[6] This step sums up the life changing acceptance of Jesus as Savior discussed in the last chapter. Yet, it does no harm to reiterate this step's importance. It will be impossible to have any success in the battle at all if one has not started this relationship with Christ. *Salvation is the prerequisite of a holy life.*

"The **second** step toward entire sanctification is entire consecration—a complete and unconditional abandonment of yourself and your all to God."[7] Philippians 2:7a recounts how Christ made himself nothing so that he might follow the will of God which results in our salvation; in like manner, we must submit ourselves fully to God. James agrees with this by stating;

> Submit yourselves, then, to God. Resist the devil, and he will flee from you. Come near to God and he will come near to you. Wash your hands, you sinners, and purify your hearts, you double-minded. (James 4:7)

Personally, I like Ruth's phrase "complete and unconditional abandonment of yourself and your all to God." (see footnote) Although raised in the holiness tradition, I did not fully come to understand this

---

[6]C.W. Ruth, *Entire Sanctification Explained* (Kansas City, Beacon Hill Press), 40.

[7]Ruth, 41

concept until I had actually served as pastor of a holiness church myself for several years. I had been trying to approach God through my knowledge or my good works. Being a pastor, it was easy for me to assume that my works, preaching, teaching, and providing pastoral care, were enough; if I just worked long enough and hard enough at "church" work, then I must be "OK" in God's eyes. I know many who similarly try to approach God through their giving or their charisma. Unfortunately all of these methods are doomed to failure if the goal is a holy life. The purity of heart and the infusion of light and the Holy Spirit cannot come through our own righteousness, no matter how "good" the works, how skilled the sermon, or how much the donation.

The reason for this is quite simple when you think about it. God, being God, has everything we have, or imagine, in an abundance which paupers us. We cannot begin to match Him in any area. Thus, when we try to "prove" our worthiness by doing or giving what He already has, we are in reality trying to persuade him how valuable we are to Him and provide reasons why He should fill us with the light of the Holy Spirit. The idea that we can do anything worthy of salvation or sanctification reduces Jesus' sacrifice to a meaningless gesture.

There is a place for works of righteousness, but not as a way to earn God's mercy or salvation. Indeed the works of righteousness have their place as a *result* of our love for Him, *not* as a means to manipulate God into filling our lives with His presence. No, the rightness of His presence comes when we allow our weaknesses, faults, insecurities, and fears to fall before the Lord in [91]"complete and unconditional abandonment." God's use of these individuals has changed the course of our world time after time because they refused to be strong in their own sight, acknowledging instead their weaknesses and trusting in God.

This truth is probably the most profound and hardest truth in the world. It is when we are weakest that we have the greatest potential for strength and power, because it is when we are weakest that we are dependant upon the omnipotence of God. Discussing this second step, Ruth elaborates:

> "Usually there are three stages or steps before consecration is completed.
>
>   1. 'I desire to consecrate.'
>
>   2. 'I am trying to consecrate.'
>
>   3. 'I do give up all to Jesus.'"[8]

The actuality of such consecration, while only possible after the salvation, may come moments after that conversion, or may take months or years. Acts 19:1-7 is indicative that the baptism of the Holy Spirit does not necessarily follow immediately upon salvation. This can also be seen in Acts 10 and the experience at Cornelius' house. Both references, however, support the definite crisis aspect of the experience. Sanctification, or the baptism of the Holy Spirit, is a crisis experience which occurs at a specific point, yet requires a process to get to that point and a different, ongoing process for continued victory afterwards. This is the ongoing battle for the

---

[8]Ruth, 41

heart. Satan is fully aware that consecration is vital to the warrior's effectiveness and without this step the warrior will live in a *twilight zone*, part way into the light and part way into the darkness. This twilight zone always leaves the warrior struggling, sickly, and devoid of power. You are a child of God as long as you maintain your salvation (i.e. your faith in God as savior and Lord and a continuation of a repentant lifestyle). However, without the infilling power of the Holy Spirit which comes through sanctification, much of the warrior's time and effectiveness will be spent in maintaining that repentant lifestyle on his own strength. The believer needs the presence of the Holy Spirit to rise above and defeat the demons which strive continually to persuade him to let slide his spiritual maintenance until the warrior is once again trapped in his foul prison. This battle is real. Satan does not want you to completely abandon yourself to Christ for the very reason cited by Mr. Frangipane at the first of this chapter, "...because in the very areas where he once had access, there stands the Lord, and Satan is terrified of Jesus Christ."[9] Sanctification is the process of setting aside something for a holy use. For the warrior, sanctification is the abandonment of all that he is, so that he may be used solely for God's holy purposes. Thus, Peter's admonition to be holy in 1 Peter 1:15 is fulfilled through the abandonment of self to the will of God.

Ruth's **third** step to obtaining the infilling of the Holy Spirit is a seal which denies Satan the access he had before.

---

[9]Frangipane, 9

Third. When the foregoing steps have been taken--so that there is no lingering doubt regarding those points, it only remains for the seeker to exercise a little faith--appropriating faith--which appropriates the promises and receives the blessing God has promised. Faith is simply believing what God says, and believing it because God said it, and so making the promise our own. We may encourage our faith by determining the following three points: 1. God is able to sanctify me holy. 2. God is willing to sanctify me wholly. 3. God is ready to sanctify me wholly. If God is now able, willing, and ready to sanctify me wholly, and I am willing and ready to be sanctified wholly, what is to hinder? I can, and I will, and I do believe that Jesus sanctifies one wholly. I have done my part, I now believe He does His part. My case is wholly in His hands: I now trust Jesus to sanctify me wholly. I do now receive Jesus as my Sanctifier, and trust His blood to cleanse my heart form all sin.[10]

This is a significant step for the spiritual warrior. Now Jesus is acknowledged commander of my life in every area.

Questions:

1. Summarize each of C.W. Ruth's steps leading to entire sanctification.

2. What does "unconditional abandonment of yourself and your all to God" mean to you personally?

ON-GOING PROCESS

What sanctification accomplishes in the life of the warrior.

While I have noted the steps that lead the warrior to sanctification, I feel we need to touch on what is accomplished for the warrior through

---

[10]Ruth, 41

sanctification. Jesus told His disciples to wait in Jerusalem until the Holy Spirit came (Acts 1:8). They did just that and on the day of Pentecost as they were praying together in Jerusalem the power of the Holy Spirit was made real to them and the world in a powerful way.

> When the day of Pentecost came, they were all together in one place. Suddenly a sound like the blowing of a violent wind came from heaven and filled the whole house where they were sitting. They saw what seemed to be tongues of fire that separated and came to rest on each of them. Acts 2:1-4

The effects of sanctification have been described by many authors, but we will touch on the points suggested by William Greathouse, one of the great holiness authors and preachers of the twentieth century. He shares four effects. To be baptized with the Holy Spirit:

1. is to be purified in heart.

2. is to be empowered.

3. is to be stamped with the image of Christ.

4. is to be Spirit-filled.[11]

These four areas sum up the change in nature and capabilities of the warrior and are described in greater detail below.

---

[11]Ruth, 41

*1.   To be baptized with the Holy Spirit is to be **purified in Heart***

The heart is purged of the old nature which desires my way and my rights more than God's will for my life. Where before his motives were directed by a nature that sought the satisfaction of self, now the warrior's heart is focused on satisfying the will of God. Where before the carnal, sinful nature suggested doing things "my" way, now the warrior seeks to do things God's way. This purging may be likened to taking an old rusty pot and scouring with a cleanser until it shines. It may be likened to metal which must be melted by the fire to remove any contaminating source. It is hard to imagine how the pot feels when it is scrubbed, or how the metal feels when it is fired to the melting point. We cannot totally relate to inanimate objects but we can imagine the scrubbing or the heat and understand that this cleansing of the old nature from our lives might not be comfortable. The purging may also be likened to the cleansing of a wound with antiseptic. I remember when I would come home with scrapes and small cuts. My mom would gently wash away the dirt. The wound looked clean to me, but then she got out the "red stuff." That red-stuff was the antiseptic which destroyed the germs which could cause infection. When she applied it to my scrape the pain was intense and to my small mind even greater than the pain caused by the scrape. The power of the Holy Spirit sweeps into our soul to cleanse out that old nature which continues to cause us to stumble and fall. Like the red stuff cleansing the deep, un-seeable germs, the Holy Spirit cleanses the old man inside each of us which, if left un-cleansed, causes infection and death. Remember, salvation was never meant to stand alone. We were always meant to have the support of the Holy Spirit in the battle.

2.   *To be baptized with the Holy Spirit is be **empowered***

The Holy Spirit empowers the warrior. After struggling in the twilight zone just to stay alive, now the warrior has power to consistently overcome temptation and advance against the enemy by bearing spiritual fruit (Galatians 6:22-25) for the cause of Christ. Not only this, but the empowering of the Holy Spirit enables the warrior to accomplish much through the exercise of his spiritual gifts and the wielding of spiritual weapons. The world enjoys portraying Christianity as weak and insipid. For some reason we have allowed this, in spite of the power available to us as children of the most high God. It is time the church and the warriors of the kingdom realize that we have all the power of heaven and earth at our disposal. We must take authority in its use instead of shying away from it. We must proclaim the salvation of Christ with accompanying signs, wonders and miracles. There is no doubt that such was Christ's intent all along. John 14:12,13 reads,

> I tell you the truth, anyone who has faith in me will do what I have been doing. He will do even greater things than these, because I am going to the Father. And I will do whatever you ask in my name, so that the Son may bring glory to the Father. You may ask me for anything in my name, and I will do it.

Christ's promise has been ignored by the church for too long. For the sanctified warrior there is real power available.

*3. To be baptized with the Holy Spirit is to be **stamped with the Image of Christ***

Being stamped with the image of Christ describes the infilling power of God's love. As Christ was able to extend love even to those who nailed Him to the cross, so the Holy Spirit enables us to love. This love is not erotic or even brotherly, as love is commonly understood by the world. Instead it is a deep compassion for others that manifests in action.

Some have said that I walk like my dad, or that I look like him. One of my sons is now being accused of that same thing about me. I like that. I love my father, and I am proud that my son looks a little like me, even if that's not a compliment. How much more wonderful if people were to point out that I show love like my Heavenly Father. *Being stamped in the image of Christ, means expressing love.* It means being an extension of Love to the world. Now, let's face it, there are a lot of people who don't know Jesus at all who are more pleasant to be around than some "Christians." The reason for this is the infilling power of the Holy Spirit is not present and/or there are demonic strongholds in place which have been accepted as normal but are in reality perversions of the true nature God gives to the sanctified. These strongholds will be discussed more fully later. If the warrior is truly filled with the Spirit of Christ, he will be more loving, not because of his own power of will, but because of the love of Christ. It seems that some of the people you and I come into contact with are jerks. They are the un-loveables of this world, and to the world at large they are left unloved. Because the warrior is taking on the image of Jesus, he will find himself responding even to these individuals differently. The Holy Spirit does make a difference. Paul writes of love in 1 Corinthians 13. He describes a love that sets a standard for what true love is, yet, it is only achievable through the power of God's love filling the warrior and stamping the image of Christ's love upon His life.

4.   *To be baptized with the Holy Spirit is to be **Spirit Filled***

The filling power of the Spirit is, perhaps, the best of all. Through the filling of the Holy Spirit we have direct fellowship with God. The warrior is never alone in the darkest night or the fiercest battle, for the Holy Spirit is by his side as a comfort and a support. David cries, "Do not cast me from your presence or take your Holy Spirit from me." (Psalm 51:11). Surely this is the cry of the warrior as well. The presence of the Holy Spirit is a guide in life's decisions, a companion in times of discouragement, and a support in the battle. His presence is the difference between victory and failure. Each one faces the "valley of the shadow of death" upon occasion. There are times when it seems as if the whole world has deserted you and you are alone. Jesus' promise that He would never leave us or forsake us is fulfilled in the abiding presence of the Holy Spirit. To those around us this presence seems nothing more than a "mind game," yet to the warrior, His presence is life and breath.

One might be tempted to stop here, as many have done, and go no farther, yet as C. Neil Strait points out:

"The sanctified life needs the same intensity that is exercised before consecration. Here is where some fall. Alter they are sanctified they slack off on their devotional life. This makes them vulnerable to Satan's attack. Sanctification does not equip us to be more self-sufficient. it puts us under the control of the Spirit whose resources are our strength.[12]

Summary

The experience of salvation and sanctification have only been lightly touched on in these chapters. If you have more questions about either experience I have included a bibliography which contains references dealing with both experiences more thoroughly than discussed here.

The next chapters provide strategies and tactics that are helpful in the battle both before and after the crisis of sanctification. In each case the effect of the strategy or tactic is multiplied by the warrior's total submission and abandonment to sanctification. Too many warriors have attempted the battle without the infilling power of the Holy Spirit only to become frustrated and defeated. With the Holy Spirit it is possible to move into new areas, to expand the territory of God in our soul, instead of maintaining the twilight zone. Now we are operating from a stronghold of light.

---

[12]C.Neil Strait, *To Be Holy* (Kansas City, Beacon Hill Press), 58

Questions:

1. How is humility a "back-door" approach to sanctification?
2. What is the first step toward sanctification and why is it first?
3. How does good works fit into the sanctified life?
4. The purging of the old nature by the Holy Spirit may be likened to the purifying of metal through melting. What effect has this "fire" had in your life?

CHAPTER 4
THE WEAPONS OF OUR WARFARE

"For though we live in the world, we do not wage war as the world does. The weapons we fight with are not the weapons of the world. On the contrary, they have divine power to demolish strongholds." (2 Corinthians 10:3-4)

Our weapons are not those of physical warfare; yet they are weapons! As every soldier knows, before any weapon can be used effectively, the body must be trained and strengthened to support the weapon's weight and make full use of its capabilities. Additional training is required for correct and accurate application of the weapon. In the military, soldiers are introduced to their weapons and, through actual practice situations, are brought to a level of competency in the use of those weapons. Powerful weapons in the hands of the untrained often do more harm than good. For the spiritual weapons described in this chapter to provide you with the optimum effectiveness, it is imperative:

First - Take spiritual weapons seriously as weapons. This book might make for nice casual reading, but the real intent of this chapter is to place within your grasp powerful weapons which have "divine power to demolish strongholds" (strongholds will be discussed more fully in chapter 8) The extent to which you take these weapons seriously will affect your abilities against demonic strongholds.

Second - Practice the use of each weapon at every opportunity. It is practice which makes an average athlete above average. It is practice which makes the musician a virtuoso. It is practice which makes a soldier a marksman. Understand which weapon you are using, why you are using that weapon instead of another, and how you can use it to your fullest potential. There are five basic weapons of spiritual warfare: They are:

- Praise

- Prayer

- Perseverance

- Perspective

- Performance.

These are the weapons for the battleground of the heart. That there are other spiritual weapons is without question but it is these weapons which will provide victory for the heart.

PRAISE

In his life changing look at praise and worship, *Worship His Majesty*, Jack Hayford clearly sets forth the principles of praise and how it enlivens the soul. "Worship," he writes, "is an opportunity for man to invite God's power and presence to move among those worshipping Him."[13] Using the

---

[13]Jack W. Hayford. Worship His Majesty (Waco, TX, Word Books, 1987). 152.

weapon of praise the warrior actually invites God to come into his life as a wellspring of peace and joy. Praise also is effective in routing the forces of darkness which attempt to prey upon our consciousness. 2 Chronicles 20:20-23 describes a setting where praise was effective in overcoming an impossibly large army.

> "Early in the morning they left for the Desert of 'Tekoa. As they set out, Jehoshaphat stood and said, 'Listen to me, Judah and people of Jerusalem! Have faith in the Lord your God and you will be upheld; have faith in His prophets and you will be successful.' After consulting the people, Jehoshaphat appointed men to sing to the Lord and to praise Him for the splendor of His holiness as they went out at the head of the army, saying: 'Give thanks to the Lord, for His love endures forever.' As they began to sing and praise, the Lord set ambushes against the men of Ammon and Moab and Mount Seir who were invading Judah, and they were defeated. The men of Ammon and Moab rose up against the men from Mount Seir to destroy and annihilate them. After they finished slaughtering the men from Seir, the helped to destroy one another."

The song of praises to God on the lips of those who desire victory in their lives unleashes God's power in miraculous ways. Note that in the passage quoted above, men were specifically appointed "to sing to the Lord and praise Him for the splendor of His holiness." These men marched at the head of a military force going out to face overwhelming odds. If anything, they should have been depressed and distressed. Their song of praise at this point became a testimony of faith in God, and God prevailed.

King David felt that praises to God were so important it is recorded (1 Chronicles 23:5) he appointed 4,000 to praise God with musical instruments he had made just for that purpose. Many of the Psalms may be attributed to David's passion to praise and worship God. Scripture abounds with examples of how praise has brought victory out of defeat. It also contains numerous admonitions to praise God. For the spiritual warrior, praise to God is a weapon which must become as natural as breath itself.

In true, sincere praise, we focus our thoughts and energies, both vocal and physical, upon glorifying God. Praise is an attitude of the heart which seeks to glorify God. It's most powerful expressions are seen in a "speaking forth." Although there is a time and a place for silent praise and worship, great power is unleashed when praise is expressed aloud in voice and physical expression. Even as I write this I realize the traditions of many churches have moved away from what is labeled "emotional outbursts" in favor of a more civilized and sedate form of worship. For those the practice of "speaking forth" may be perceived as an optional application of the weapon of Praise. This is NOT true, in fact, the reverse is actually encouraged by scripture.

> Psalm 47:1 "Clap your hand, all you nations; shout to God with cries of joy."
>
> Psalm 66:1 "Shout with joy to God, all the earth? Sing the glory of his name; make his praise glorious."
>
> Psalm 95:1,2 "Come let us sing for joy to the Lord; let us shout aloud to the Rock of our salvation. Let us come before him with thanksgiving and extol him with music and song."
>
> Isaiah 12:6 "Shout aloud and sing for joy, people of Zion, for great is the Holy One of Israel among you."

Just as David danced in the streets in joy before the Lord, so the warrior must be willing to praise God openly and without embarrassment. "Speaking forth" praises may take various forms and all should be practiced by the warrior. Examples of "speaking forth" include:

   A. Singing.

Singing is a particularly strong form of praise. As one begins to sing God's praises, his heart begins to refocus itself away from the circumstances of life and tune in to the Holy Spirit.

> Psalm 98:4-6 "Shout for joy to the Lord, all the earth, burst into jubilant song with music; make music to the Lord with the harp, with the harp and the sound of singing, with trumpets and the blast of the ram's horn--shout for joy before the Lord, the King."

> Psalm 100:1 "Shout for joy to the Lord all the earth."

> Psalm 147: 1 "Praise the Lord. How good it is to sing praises to our God, how pleasant and fitting to praise him!"

> Psalm 149:1,2 "Praise the Lord. Sing to the Lord a new song, his praise in the assembly of the saints. Let Israel rejoice in their Maker; let the people of Zion be clad in their King."

It is neither the quality nor the style of the song, but the *intent of the heart* which makes singing a weapon against evil (Psalm 63:3, 5, 66:3, 17). Some will insist on specific styles of singing as being more pleasing to God than others. There is no support, however, for such opinions. In fact those who express such strong opinions in support of one style to the detriment of another is often bigoted on other points as well. *Any music which seeks to glorify God is acceptable to God,* although clearly, certain styles will appeal to some more than others. That is one reason for different worship styles and different denominations. Different types of music resonate with different people: from classic to rock, from rap to country and EVERYTHING in between. There is no one sound God prefers over another, as long as it is sincere worship, however, there will almost certainly be one YOU prefer over another. That's OK, as long as you don't allow your personal preference to dictate to others. Instead, focus on finding your own voice and style and then worship with all your heart.

  B. Testimony.

Testimonies of God's victories, when voiced aloud accomplish three things: First it reminds me that God did work in my life. I need to be reminded; my memory is not short but life tends to continually push the past away. By voicing testimony of God's work in my life I establish it as significant. Read through the Bible and you will find it full of reminders of how God had worked in the lives of His people.

> Psalm 16:2 "I said to the Lord, 'You are my Lord; apart from you I have no good thing.'"
>
> Psalm 40:2,3 "He lifted me out of the slimy pit, out of the mud and mire; he set my feet on a rock and gave me a firm place to stand. He put a new song in my mouth, a hymn of praise to our God."
>
> Psalm 150:1,2 "Praise the Lord. Praise God in his sanctuary; praise him in his mighty heavens. Praise him for his acts of power; praise him for his surpassing greatness."

We seem to need reminders to keep our focus on what is possible. Second, as a counselor told me when I was a camper at children's camp, "testifying gives the Devil a black eye." By proclaiming what God did, we deny Satan any part of our victory and actually own up to a higher allegiance. Third, my testimonies are available for the Holy Spirit to use as examples for others who are struggling. It is one thing to be preached to, but when we know someone has been where we are and come through, it gives hope that we too will make it. No testimony...and the example is lost.

C. *Claiming the future.*

Vocally claiming future victories in God's name (e.g. the specific answer to prayer) solidifies my faith in His power and ability and thwarts Satan's attempts to make me despair or doubt.

> Psalm 62:5-8 "Find rest, 0 my soul, in God alone; my hope comes from him. He alone is my rock and my salvation; he is my fortress, I will not be shaken. My salvation and honor depend on God; he is my mighty rock, my refuge. Trust in him at all times, Oh people; pour out your hearts to him, for God is our refuge."

We are too often hesitant to claim victories ahead of time lest we be disappointed when the situation doesn't resolve as we think it should. It expresses supreme confidence to take God at His word and hold to the promises of the word. Trust in God to work all things out according to His perfect will.

D. *Words of Praise/Affirmation.*

Voicing words of praise or affirmation such as "Hosanna,""Hallelujah,""Praise the Lord,""Glory to God,""Amen," etc. continually refocuses my energies on the battle. Spoken in response to answered prayer, during the worship service as agreement to a song or the spoken word, may have gone out of fashion in many churches, however, there is no doubt that such expressions strengthen the warrior's resolve and the resolve of some who hear. If you doubt that this is so, make this your practice for a month or more and see how much greater a blessing you receive as you worship. As one who has heard such words spoken in support while preaching, I can tell you it also encourages the speaker. I'm confident that the only reason I made it through my first sermon was the speaking forth of words of agreement and encouragement from the congregation.

Speaking forth God's praises from a sincere heart brings the soul into the presence of God. Our praise helps us to mount the hill of the Lord as the Psalms of the Old Testament did for those who approached Jerusalem at the time of the Passover. By our praise we honor the sovereignty of God and proclaim our faith in His compassion and love. The praise of our lips, freely made, gives perspective to our problems and concerns, and helps us to submit them to the Lord. God accepts our praises as a sacrifice. Hebrews 13:15 admonishes us to "continually offer to God a sacrifice of praise--the fruit of lips that confess His name."

> Psalm 19:14 "May the words of my mouth and the meditation of my heart be pleasing in your sight, 0 Lord, my Rock and my Redeemer."

> Psalm 24:3-4 "Who may ascend the hill of the Lord? Who may stand in his holy place? He who has clean hands and a pure heart, who does not lift up his soul to an idol or swear by what is false."

Practice praise in worship in your own life. Sing your hymns and choruses from your heart, both in worship services and at home. Be ready to speak forth an Amen or "Praise the Lord" as a praise to God during the worship service. Let this attitude of praise carry over into your life outside the church. Continually, scripture says, not just while at church. Let your heart learn this lesson well. Heartfelt praise is powerful in spiritual warfare.

E. Physical Expression.

Another form of praise is that of physical expression. These expressions include raised hands, clapping, playing instruments, and dancing.

> Psalm 47:1 "Clap your hands, all you nations; shout to God with cries of joy."

> Psalm 134:2 "Lift up your hands in the sanctuary and praise the Lord."

> Psalm 149:3 "Let them praise his name with dancing and make music to him with tambourine and harp."

> Psalm 150:3-5 "Praise him with the sounding of the trumpet, praise him with the harp and the lyre, praise him with tambourine and dancing, praise him with the strings and flute, praise him with the clash of cymbals, praise him with resounding cymbals."

Our praise goes forth as we actually perform these actions, regardless of the views of those who are around us. Probably, this area of praise is shunned by the holiness tradition more and more due to unfortunate negative comparisons with the charismatic movement. This is particularly sad since the heritage of the holiness church always included with such visible demonstrations of praise. We have shied away from such expressions, perhaps, because we are afraid of being stamped as radicals or crazy. Well I remember the days growing up when it was common to see hands raised in praise to God and occasionally someone would be so overcome by the power of the Spirit of God that they would begin to run around the sanctuary praising God. Sadly, unless we open ourselves to the Spirit as He would manifest Himself, not just as we will allow Him to be manifested, an integral part of our praise will be lost and with it part of the power which comes through this weapon. How many times, I wonder, are we kept from God's fullest blessing because of our reluctance to "look foolish" before men. The spiritual warrior who desires complete victory will begin to retrain himself into new habits of praise that include both verbal and physical expressions of glorifying God.

Praise is a result of our love for God but its practice must be consciously cultivated. The power of God released by praise has the ability to heal, encourage, strengthen and overcome. It is one of the warrior's most used weapons.

Questions:

1. Which of the different aspects of praise comes easiest to you?
2. Which is more difficult and why?
3. What could you do to stretch yourself to practice at least one additional form of Praise?

PRAYER

Prayer is connecting with God. It is the connection which builds the relationship. If praise is the entry into God's presence, then prayer is the actual interaction between man and God. According to Strait, "Prayer is the number one discipline. Prayer is the breathing of the soul--the talking and listening to God that is so vital."[14] For the warrior, a consistent, on

---

[14]Strait, p. 29.

purpose, prayer life is non-negotiable. It is here that God begins to teach the soul and provide guidance in the circumstances of life. It is in prayer, and God's revelations through prayer, that we are moved closer and closer to the ideal that God has for us.

Yet, this type of prayer is probably foreign to our limited understanding and experiences. For the warrior, prayer starts, as all training does, as an arduous task that leaves the warrior sore, weak, and frustrated. The discipline of prayer is misunderstood to be boring on the one hand or too insightful on the other, and so is often pushed out of a busy schedule with only a twinge of guilt. Disciplining oneself to consistency here is one of the hardest, yet one of the most productive of tasks. Slocum writes,

> "The first discipline for developing the spiritual dimension of the heart, then, is making time to 'keep in touch' daily. The spiritual dimension of my heart develops when I come each day as a sinner saved by grace into the forgiving, renewing presence of Christ. Without this daily contact, I drift into the role of high-tech hypocrite."[15]

Daniel, one of my heroes, even though a busy leader and a counselor to the King, made time three times a day to pray to God. Martin Luther made it a point to rise early and pray and, if the schedule was especially busy, to add even more time to pray. The warrior must be a man or woman of prayer. Without these communication channels being open to God at all times, it will be difficult, if not impossible, to hear Him speak when He needs to warn or reveal a new truth.

---

[15]Robert E. Slocum. *Maximize Your Ministry* (Colorado Springs, NavPress, 1990), 152.

Were all this not enough, God's word commands that we "pray without ceasing." (1 Thessalonians 5:17) Other texts, such as Luke 21:36 ("Be always on the watch, and pray...") from the mouth of Jesus Himself, are constant reminders of the importance of prayer.

Larry Lea's insightful book, *Could You Not Tarry One Hour?* indicates that while the discipline of prayer begins as a wearisome chore, with patient persistence it becomes a habit and finally a joy.[16] E.M. Bounds adds," Praying is spiritual work, and nature does not like taxing, spiritual work. Human nature wants to sail to heaven under a pleasant breeze, and a full, smooth sea."[17]

The serious warrior will mark a specific block of time each day for this communion with God, usually not less than thirty minutes each day; many will find an hour too short as the relationship grows. However, this should not become a legalistic task measured by the clock. Nor should this be an exercise in pagan babblings as Jesus warns against in Matthew 6, but a deep, on-purpose, contact with the Creator, the Provider, the Holy Redeeming God. To attempt to shorten this time is to deprive the soul of the one source of "vitamins' necessary for continued health."Little praying is a kind of make-believe, a salve for the conscience, a farce and a delusion." writes Bounds.[18]

---

[16] Larry Lea, Could You Not Tarry One Hour.

[17] E.M. Bounds. Power Through Prayer (Springdale, PA, Whitaker House, 1982), 36.

[18] Bounds, p.36.

Although there are several "parts" of prayer and different styles of prayer and kinds of prayers, warfare prayer is largely directed at intercession and petition. Intercession is "standing in the gap" for another's spiritual need. Petition, especially for revival and a greater desire for the things of God on the part of the warrior, sets the Spirit free to start a fire that destroys demonic influence. I challenge you to begin your time of prayer immediately. If the warrior will set aside time for conversation and communion with God, then God will honor and bless that warrior. Hebrews 5:7 indicates that Jesus' prayers and petitions were heard specifically because they were offered in reverent submission. Cornelius' regular praying is cited in Acts 10:4 as a major reason for God's notice, which ultimately led to the spread of the gospel to the gentiles. 2 Chronicles 7:14 declares if we will humble ourselves and turn from our wicked ways, God will hear us and answer us. Jeremiah 29:13 cites God as saying that if we seek him with all our hearts he will be found.

The greatest problem we face is our inability to focus on anything for very long, much less prayer. Strait quotes Adam Clark as advising: "Pray much in private. Without this you will find it utterly impossible to keep yourself in the love of God."[19] This I have personally found to be true.

To seek God with all the heart will sometimes require fasting. Fasting is a spiritual discipline which can yield amazing results. Fasting, simply put, is doing without something (usually food) for a specific period

---

[19]Strait, p. 30.

of time. It is usually coupled with a focused time of prayer for a particular concern. Fasting may be one meal or several days. It may be directed at food or specific foods. It is not a diet, nor should it be used as such. Fasting is a time honored and scripture approved method of focus.

The warrior who wishes to move past the battle for the heart and on into warfare in heavenly realms will become well acquainted with this weapon of warfare. One method which bears much fruit and strengthens the warriors capability with this weapon is to compose a list of individuals who need God. Take that list to God, calling each name and need out before him. Repeat this in sincerity, whether fasting or not as often as it comes to mind, at least daily for a designated period of time, 50 - 60 days works well, however, in some cases perseverance in this area over years can bear much fruit. Record your requests in a journal and as God answers, highlight the requests. As you remain focused on these requests, you will begin to see God answer prayers and perform miracles. You will also experience some serious spiritual attacks. Satan does not want anyone to pray at this level of consistency. These attacks are why the next weapon, perseverance, must be studied and ready.

Questions:

1. Discuss the practical implications of what it would mean for the average person to "pray without ceasing."
2. Describe you current prayer life and how it is or is not equipping you for facing the challenges in your life.

PERSEVERANCE

The actions of some might indicate that there is a seniority system for the children of God; that once you reach a certain age it is quite understandable if you want to retire from active Christian service and "let the young people take over." This myth has caused some saints to slow down their services of love, come to a gentle stop, and then slowly pull away from God altogether. Others, abusing the Calvinist doctrines, use the "once saved, always saved" phraseology to validate a lifestyle totally opposed to God's word.

Perseverance is a no-stop attitude. It is a mental orientation that refuses to give up. Paul said,

> "Forgetting what is behind and straining toward what is ahead, I press on toward the goal to win the prize for which God has called me heavenward in Christ Jesus." (Philippians 3: 13b-14).

In spiritual warfare, the main objective of the enemy is not to destroy you--he has all eternity for that, it is to make you give up your walk with Christ. We will discuss his methods of attack later, but suffice it for now to say that the warrior must be committed to the long-haul--even when it looks as if the situation is hopeless. God's word supports a persevering spirit.

> 1 Corinthians 15:58 "Therefore, my dear brothers, stand firm. Let nothing move you. Always give yourselves fully to the work of the Lord, because you know that your labor in the Lord is not in vain."

> 1 Corinthians 16: 13-14 "Be on your guard; stand firm in the faith; be men of courage; be strong. Do everything in love."

Galatians 5:1"It is for freedom that Christ has set us free. Stand firm, then, and do not let yourselves be burdened again by a yoke of slavery."

2 Thessalonians 2:15 "So then, brothers, stand firm and hold to the teachings we passed on to you, whether by word of mouth or by letter."

Hebrews 3:14 "We have come to share in Christ if we hold firmly till the end the confidence we had at first."

James 5:8"You too, be patient and stand firm, because the Lord's coming is near."

These texts and others are cited fully so that you will have the full impact of God's word on the importance of standing firm, of persevering. Satan's demonic forces are doing their best to cut you off from God and life.

Willy (fictitious name of an actual character) and his wife Willamay were two of the nicest people you would want to meet. They would give you anything they had and if they knew you had a need, they did their best to respond. As I got to know Willy and Willamay, I appreciated their kind spirits, but it wasn't long before I discovered that their commitment to Christ was not as intense as their commitment to people's needs. When trauma entered their lives, the first thing to go was God. "How could a loving God allow this to happen?" or "Why us God?" Their level of spiritual maturity never grew above the most basic levels. Their service to others was marred by a deficiency so common today: godlessness. During the good times and the easy times they wanted to follow the Lord and His will for their lives but when faced with crisis, or even a busy schedule, those words were left hanging in the air as they struggled with the enemy without the power of God.

The weapon of perseverance may be likened to a foundation or a large rock. It is that upon which we build everything else. A marriage only works when there is a commitment from each partner "for as long as we both shall live." To waver on such commitment is to admit that there exists reasons why it is OK to quit. God is steadfast in His commitment, but are we? The same is true with our relationship with Jesus Christ. The foundation is a wholesale, sold out, commitment which refuses to acknowledge any reason for quitting. Romans 8:35ff shares the resolve of Paul to allow nothing to separate him from God's love:

> "Who shall separate us from the love of Christ? Shall trouble or hardship or persecution or famine or nakedness or danger or sword? As it is written:' For your sake we face death all day long; we are considered as sheep to be slaughtered. 'No in all these things we are more than conquerors through him who loved us. For I am convinced that neither death nor life, neither angels nor demons, neither the present nor the future, nor any powers, neither height nor depth, nor anything else in all creation, will be able to separate us from the love of God that is in Christ Jesus our Lord."

> "I recall a university student who encountered the claims of Jesus and, on the spot, committed his life to Christ. He returned to his usual routine in the dorm, classroom, and social life. After a few weeks, he met with his Christian counselor, who asked him how things were going. He said, 'It's like there is a black dog and a white dog inside my life and they are fighting all the time.' The counselor asked him which one was winning. The student thought a moment and replied mater-of-factly (sic), 'The one I feed the most.'"[20]

Consider your commitment to "feed" the presence of God within you. Too many seek to dabble in the edges of sin, seeking how far they can go toward sin without losing their soul. The warriors perspective is

---

[20]Slocum, p. 125.

entirely opposite. It is a seeking of how far *away* from sin and *toward* God can one go. If the warrior has a perspective which sees the battle in spiritual terms he has a handle on victory. Seen from this angle, the battle may be won or avoided. 1 Corinthians 10:13 asserts there is always a way of escape if the battle is too intense. Scripture also assures us that if we resist Satan, he must flee. The weapon of perseverance is, therefore, crucial to any victory. There will always be temptations to quit, or at least not try so hard.

Take time to examine your own life in the light of the weapon of perseverance. What would it take for you to give up? Would it take a divorce, personal tragedy, financial troubles, death of a loved one? Taking time to consider all that might happen and deciding ahead of time that nothing will separate you from God's love will assist you when in the valley of the shadow of death. The warrior who wields the weapon of perseverance will always be a threat to Satan. The willingness to stand firm, whatever the need and not falter under enemy fire is invaluable. Developing this weapon requires maturity and character which sees a bigger picture and fights for that end. James admonishes us with these words:

> "Consider it pure joy, my brothers, whenever you face trials of many kinds, because you know that the testing of your faith develops perseverance. Perseverance must finish its work so that you may be mature and complete, not lacking anything." James 1:2-4

> Questions:
>
> 1. Discuss this statement from the chapter: "In spiritual warfare, the main objective of the enemy is not to destroy you--he has all eternity for that, it is to make you give up your walk with Christ."
> 2. The question was asked, "what would it take for you to give up your faith?" Take a few minutes and go into some of the tragedies which could (or have) occur in you life and how you think they would impact your decision to persevere in you faith.

PERSPECTIVE

Philippians 2:5 reads, "Your attitude should be the same as that of Christ Jesus..." This matter of perspective has been written about and talked about extensively. The most common interpretation for the Christian is that offered by Norman Vincent Peal and Robert Schuller, having to do with positive or possibility thinking. A positive perspective turns defeat into victory. It allows the warrior to believe that he can do all things through Christ. Certainly the warrior must have this perspective. While the works of Schuller and Peal are significant contributions and helpful to the Christian's walk, the warrior's perspective needs one added dimension. Paul tells us:

"For our struggle is not against flesh and blood, but against the rulers, against the authorities, against the powers of this dark world and against the spiritual forces of evil in the heavenly realms." Ephesians 6:12

Clearly, our struggle is on a higher plane than we normally perceive. Training ourselves to view earthly circumstances from the perspective of spiritual warfare will bring us to the place where the *root*, and not the symptoms, of a problem are exposed and able to be treated.

The use of this weapon requires great concentration. Satan's attacks will invariably attempt to draw the warrior's consciousness away from seeing the spiritual battle and focus instead upon the physical problem. *This cannot be over emphasized.* It is so easy in the midst of trauma or pain to begin, as we have been taught to do all our lives, first to deal with the problem from an entirely human perspective, and only when it develops beyond our resources, call upon God. For the Christian, situations like fights with our spouse, difficulties with our children, temptations at work, physical illness, emotional difficulties, or financial struggles are not what they seem to be on the surface. Indeed, a right perspective will see Satanic forces trying to remove our peace and separate us from the love of God.

Saul, the first king of Israel, ran into this problem. Saul was facing a deadly enemy; his army was vastly outnumbered and things looked bleak. At that time the offering to God was to be made by God's appointed priest, Samuel. When Samuel did not respond as quickly as Saul felt was appropriate, he took matters into his own hands, without regard for spiritual battle. Samuel 13:8-14 describes the results:

"He (Saul) waited seven days, the time set by Samuel; but Samuel did not come to Gilgal, and Saul's men began to scatter. So he said, 'Bring me the burnt offering and the fellowship offerings.' and Saul offered up the burnt offering. Just as he finished making the offering, Samuel arrived, and Saul went Out to greet him. 'What have you done?' asked Samuel. Saul replied, 'When I saw that the men were scattering, and that you did not come at the set time, and that the Philistines were assembling at Micmash, I thought, now the Philistines will come down against me at Gilgal, and I have not sought the Lord's favor. So I felt compelled to offer the burnt offering.' 'You acted foolishly,' Samuel said. 'You have not kept the command the Lord your God gave you; if you had, he would have established your kingdom over Israel for all time. But now your kingdom will not endure; the Lord has sought out a man after his own heart and appointed him leader of his people because you have not kept the Lord's command.'"

The key words from this passage are "I felt compelled..." and "You have not kept the command the Lord your God gave you...." ***God never compels us to go against His word***. Such compulsions come from our own insecurities and demonic influences. If you are feeling compelled to violate God's word, beware!! Unfortunately, this tragedy is repeated in our lives. We too "feel compelled" to react in certain ways because we are unfamiliar with this powerful weapon of perspective. The battle is God's. Whenever you are in a position that is stressful, or you feel requires an immediate response--stop and get a Godly perspective and you will discover how God helps you use your weapons wisely.

This weapon has been the most significant, and most difficult for me to use. Because of personal problems my family and I went through three very difficult years, and I came close to walking away from God's call and my faith. During that time I knew nothing of the principles of spiritual warfare and the "weapon of perspective" in particular. All I could see were my problems which seemed beyond my abilities. When I would pray, my prayers focused on God magically making all my problems go away, and when they didn't, I became more frustrated. God brought me through that difficulty with the assistance of loving support from other Christians. Knowledge of the weapon of perspective would have given me insight into the larger picture and the perception to understand that my problems were not directed by the people or situations where they seemed to originate, but came from a different realm. Knowing this, I could have battled more effectively and saved myself and my family some of the stress of those days.

Its kind of like driving. Under normal conditions we have no problem seeing the road. When darkness comes, we simply switch on the lights and continue on our way. Spiritually, the analogy holds, for when obvious spiritual attacks come, our light (faith in God) cuts right through. However, it's a different story when a fog bank settles in. Suddenly the lights don't seem to work so well. We are reduced to a crawl and occasionally even a stop. Now and again accidents may be seen where others have misjudged the road and either ran off the road or into oncoming traffic. Spiritually, the fog may be likened to the circumstances of life which we do not perceive to be spiritual attacks. Because our perception is tuned to human wave lengths we attempt to deal with the circumstances from a human perspective. This is why we see so many problems in the church and so many who are spiritual casualties. The right perspective, the perspective which will bring victory sees the spiritual side of every circumstance and brings faith in God's providence into each situation.

One of the most effective lies Satan tells is that if you are living "right," you will not experience difficulties and/or trauma in your life. Even a casual reading into the life of Biblical saints and those throughout history deny such a lie. Romans 8:28 is the key verse for those whose perspective is properly focused. While it may sound trite, for those who truly know God and have faith, all things do work for their eternal good.

The military uses at least two different methods for ground troops to "see" the enemy at night. The starlight scope and the infrared scope allow the soldier to identify and aim his weapons with great accuracy in almost total darkness. The spiritual warrior's weapon of perspective may be likened to these scopes. By using the right perspective, the enemy is clearly identified and other weapons may then be brought to bear for destruction.

Question:

1. The weapon of perspective is often the most difficult to use simply because it is so difficult to keep in mind the warfare in heavenly realms when we are going through difficulty here. Discuss a time when you were able to keep this perspective as well as a time when you didn't and the difference in how it worked out.

2. What could you do to help keep the right perspective?

PERFORMANCE

It is said that in the church 20% of the people do 80% of the work. I can support those statistics from my years in the ministry. It is ever so much easier to worship and praise the Lord than it is to get your hands dirty working. It is much more "noble" to proclaim your standing firm in the face of trial, than to actually serve quietly where needed. People would almost always rather give money than time to ministry, although usually both are considered asking too much from busy schedules and a tight economy.

Because of this attitude, many "warrior wannabes" fall by the wayside. God never intended for the warrior to look out only for himself. Paul writes to Titus:

> "Our people must learn to devote themselves to doing what is good, in order that they may provide for daily necessities and not live unproductive lives." Titus 3:14

His sentiment here and throughout his writings is that God's people are the channels through which the gospel will reach the world. James' writings are soundly behind such a concept. James is even more strident; forcing those who claim to be Christians to examine how they are involved in the needs of those around them. James 2:14-19 proclaims:

> "What good is it, my brothers, if a man claims to have faith but has not deeds? Can such faith save him? Suppose a brother or sister is without clothes and daily food. If one of you says to him,' Go, I wish you well; keep warm and well fed,' but does nothing about his physical needs, what good is it? In the same way faith by itself, if it is not accompanied by action, is dead. But someone will say, 'You have faith; I have deeds. Show me your faith without deeds, and I will show you my faith by what I do.

You believe that there is one God. Good! Even the demons believe that--and shudder."

For James, Christianity without service is not real Christianity. God's warriors will find in their performance of works of love and service to the lost world an opportunity to represent Christ not possible in any other way. Performing actual ministry accomplishes two things:

1. It fulfills the scriptural commandments cited above.

2. It takes the love of God out of the abstract and makes it real for all to see.

John writes in his first epistle:

"This is how we know what love is: Jesus Christ laid down his life for us. And we ought to lay down our lives for our brothers. If anyone has material possessions and sees his brother in need but has no pity on him, how can the love of God be in him? Dear children, let us not love with words or tongue but with actions and in truth." John 3: 16-18.

Jesus' life was an example of this very attitude. He gave up the glory of heaven so that He might share love with us and life through His sacrifice. In spite of such examples there is still a profound lethargy amongst most of God's professed warriors to be involved in any ministry. Satan effectively draws the attention of many to themselves and their own needs and reminds them of the things they want to do, need to do, and have to do. It is only when the warrior sees his part in the mission and determines that the fulfillment of that mission is important that he will do his part.

Interestingly, the terminology of holiness indicates that one of the works of the Holy Spirit is to empower believers for works of service. That was evidenced with power on the day of Pentecost and throughout the pages of the book of Acts. In the first century, Christian response was high and there was a passion about sharing their faith. In Acts 8:1-4 we read of the persecution which came upon the church and how many were put into prison and others scattered throughout the region. Verse one indicates that the apostles stayed in Jerusalem, but we see in verse four the secret that has always been there, "Those who had been scattered preached the word wherever they went."

Today, however, it is a struggle to motivate many to even invite someone to a worship service, to say nothing about sharing one's faith. Part of the problem is due to:

- **Spectator mentality** which sees every action as entertainment or information. Sports and the media continue to foster this attitude which pervades the church. Today's worship services often are designed to compete with other churches because the desire of "warrior wannabe" has less to do with service than flashy worship.

- **Specialist thinking** which places the responsibility on someone else. The move to specialization has benefited much of our lives, yet it fosters the belief that the average Christian is not capable of ministry when there are professional ministers who can do the job and do it "right." Obviously, some ministerial functions require training to be done effectively. The tendency, however, is to do nothing at all while waiting to be trained, not even asking to be trained in the first place, thinking, "after all, if they really need me, they will approach me and get me trained," and/or "why should I ask to get involved."

- **Basic insecurities** which undermine the warrior's confidence. Although filled with the Holy Spirit, many struggle with demonic strongholds which occupy a major portion of the warrior's attention and suggest that he is not capable or worthy of ministering to others more holy than himself. These strongholds will be discussed later in this book.

- **Misunderstanding the Mission** - Probably the most significant barrier blocking Christians from active involvement in works of service is an incorrect perception of the mission which Jesus left the church. When the mission is perceived as important and worthwhile works of service naturally follow.

Of course the opposite of this weapon is the possibility that Satan might use it against us by convincing us that our salvation comes through our performance, instead of the other way around. This is a real risk an many fall prey to this, however, it seems to me that in reacting against a "works" based faith, we've "thrown the baby out with the bath water"; we ignore or lessen the value of service as a truly powerful weapon against the enemy.

Summary

The weapons which are available to a believer are not the weapons of this world, in fact they probably wouldn't be considered weapons at all.

For the unbeliever, that would be true, but when arising from a heart fully committed to Jesus Christ and living in the fullness of the Spirit, these weapons literally have the power to overcome the enemy and bring victory and joy to the believer and to the church.

Questions:

1. What is the relationship between practice and effectiveness? How does this relate to spiritual weapons.
2. Of the four roadblocks to the use of the weapon of performance, which is the most dangerous?
3. Overall, which weapon is the most difficult for you to use? Why?
4. Comment on the offensive vs defensive nature of these weapons.

CHAPTER 5
THE DEFENSIVE STANCE

Spiritual warfare waged for the heart is given many faces by the father of lies, Satan. These faces include, family strife, financial problems, physical illness, etc. The defensive stance, when properly learned and applied, enables the warrior to overcome daily temptations with confidence, no matter how those temptations are presented. While other aspects of spiritual warfare include offensive attacks on demonic strongholds, this aspect focuses upon defending oneself against the temptations that are a part of human existence. Satan tries to make us believe that Christians, "real" Christians, are above temptation. This is, of course, a lie. He presents this lie through the media, our neighbors, families, and friends with the intent to discourage the warrior and persuade her that persevering is futile. Reality is that every Christian, no matter how long they have been a Christian, is tempted at some point or another. *There are no exceptions.* The teachings of this chapter will give you the 'armor" you need to fight effectively in this battle.

The source of the defensive stance is drawn from Paul's description of spiritual armor in Ephesians 6, but is actually woven throughout God's word. The defensive stance is described by Paul in terms of armor. I believe he does this to emphasize that the factors he mentions are meant to protect vital parts of a believer's relationship with Christ.

In actual practice warriors were introduced to their armor in different ways. One of the most effective is to introduce one piece of armor at a time and have the warrior learn to live with that piece. At rest, on the run, at meals, at sleep, at weapons practice, everywhere the warrior goes that piece of armor was constantly present, until being without it was like being unclothed. As more and more pieces were added, they too became a part of the warrior's identity. The analogy here is obvious. The defensive stance of the spiritual warrior will never be achieved by merely reading about the armor. Each piece, each part of the defensive stance must be researched, prayed over, meditated upon and *consciously practiced* until the spiritual warrior unconsciously owns it. Anything less may prove fatal when temptations strike.

I wear glasses. The very first thing I reach for in the morning, and the last I lay down at night, are my glasses. They are a reflexive part of my existence. I hardly ever even give them a conscious thought, yet without them I am crippled. Just so, the defensive stance becomes a reflexive part of our very lives. Some writers suggest that we "pray" on the armor each day. I am proposing that the warrior "live" in the armor of God constantly. This means applying oneself to the discipline required to "own" our armor because there is no predicting just how, or when, Satan will strike.

PUT ON THE BELT OF TRUTH

The belt served two basic functions with a third possible depending upon how it was worn.

> "The 'belt' was not an ornament but served an essential purpose. It gathered in the short tunic and helped keep the breastplate in place when the latter was fitted on. From it hung the scabbard in which the sword was sheathed."[21]

---

[21] A. Skevington Wood, "Ephesians, " Frank E. Gaebelein, ed. *The Expositor's Bible Commentary, Volume 11* (Grand Rapids, Zondervan Publishing House, 1978), p. 87

Scripturally, the focus is not the belt, but on truth. The big question, as Pilot asked Jesus in John 18:38 is, "What is truth?" The answer is far deeper and more meaningful than you might imagine. First, the obvious: Truth has no part in lies or deception. Leviticus 19:11 records God's command on this issue very clearly: "Do not lie. Do not deceive one another." This view is upheld in the New Testament with Colossians 3:9 being only one of several references: "Do not lie to each other." Thus, as we are admonished to put on the belt of truth, we are also commanded not to lie. Yet, one person's lie could possibly be another's truth. God must have realized the possibility of twisting His commands to fit our convenience, for His word clearly identifies truth in three different ways:

1. TRUTH is the Holy Spirit.

John 14:17 identifies the Holy Spirit as the spirit of truth. No other explanation is given at that point. Dodds observes about the Holy Spirit: "He would enable them to understand the new truths which were battling with their old conceptions, and to readjust their beliefs around a new center."[22] John himself supports such a view, for in John 16:13 we read, "But when he, the Spirit of Truth, comes, he will guide you into all truth." The Holy Spirit is, therefore, presented in these passages in two roles;

A. The essence of truth, and

B. An instructor of truth.

Practically, to have such a view of the Holy Spirit makes the presence of the "belt" around us an expression of our desire to apply ourselves to learn all that we can under the Holy Spirit's guidance. It

[22]Marcus Dods, "The Gospel of St. John, " W. Robertson Nicoll, ed., *The Expositor's Greek Testament Volume One* (Grand Rapids, Wm. B. Erdmans Publishing House, reprinted 1974), p. 124.

means that we become His willing students, ever striving to know more of God's truth for our lives.

2. TRUTH is the Word.

Ephesians 1:13 says, "And you also were included in Christ when you heard the word of truth, the gospel of your salvation."

The word of truth here is synonymous with the gospel of salvation. It is the "good news" of Jesus' redemption plan for our souls. The word of truth is God's Holy Word, the Bible. If we accept the Holy Spirit as the Spirit of Truth and the Instructor of Truth, the "good news" becomes the text book for our lessons. By belting on truth we make a powerful connection with God's work throughout history for the salvation of man. We are joined, as it were, by that belt to a greater tradition, a greater faith than ours alone. Study of this truth under the Spirit's guidance will hold our armor together with sound doctrine so that it will not shift when Satan's minions strike. The word of truth holds us together when the enemy attacks.

3. TRUTH is Jesus.

John 1:17, "For the law was given through Moses; grace and truth came through Jesus Christ."

John 14:6, "Jesus answered, I am the way, and the truth, and the life, no one comes to the Father except through me."

Clearly and without hesitation, Jesus proclaims himself to be the truth. Now added to our concept of truth is the essence of Jesus as Christ. Men are sometimes identified by what they have done and the influence they leave behind. Contained in the written word is a picture and a presence of Jesus which sets before us a new and overriding truth to which all others must bow. We are admonished to put on the belt of truth. By doing so we are identifying ourselves with that truth, Jesus Christ! Thus, we become a living, breathing model of Jesus Christ to those with whom we come into contact. Don't be afraid or intimidated. God knows you aren't perfect. He knows of your problems and even in the midst of them He gives this pattern for overcoming temptations. Simply be Jesus to the best of your abilities.

Now because we are attempting to actually put on this armor, I want to employ a memory device I learned from Dr. Mendal Taylor. When you put on your belt, if you wear a belt, or pick up your purse, if you carry a purse, or just fasten your pants or skirt, make a conscious effort to remember that you also have on the belt of truth and take a moment to go over in your mind just what that means:

1. TRUTH is the Spirit.

2. TRUTH is the Word.

3. TRUTH is Jesus Christ

THE BREASTPLATE OF RIGHTEOUSNESS

The variation in breastplate design and the history of the breastplate's development fall beyond the scope of this work. We are more concerned with the function of the breastplate. What was it designed to do? Stated in the simplest possible terms: the breastplate protects the vital organs from injury. Thus a spiritual breastplate would have as it's purpose the protection of the spiritually vital organs.

The most important "vital organ" from a spiritual point of view has to do with the warrior's relationship with Christ. A strong and healthy warrior will have a solid bond with Jesus. A weak and wounded warrior will not. That relationship is the difference between life and death. It must be protected at all costs!

Protection of this vital organ is going to require some pretty heavy material. Although there is plenty of material from which to form the breastplate throughout the Old and New Testaments, 1 Peter gives us necessary details on breastplate construction.1 Peter 2:12 provides the supporting framework on which the rest hangs:

> "Live such good lives among the pagans, that though they accuse you of doing wrong, they may see our good deeds and glorify God on the day he visits you."

Live a good life. What a powerful statement. Don't mess around the edges of right and wrong. Don't dabble in the grays. One of the greatest dangers facing Christians today is the seeming lack of clear cut good and bad, right and wrong. Too many rationalize saying, "The simply bad is not as bad as the very bad but not quite as good as the slightly bad, therefore, while I may not be very good, I'm still not very bad, even though I practice the slightly bad. In fact, since I'm not doing the very bad, I must be doing good." This confusing line of reasoning, fostered in our warfare by the Father of Lies, undermines the effectiveness of the breastplate to protect our relationship with Christ.

Other passages from 1 Peter make up the actual construction of this important piece of our defense.

> I Peter 2:1 Therefore rid yourselves of all malice and all deceit, hypocrisy, envy, and slander of every kind

This passage speaks to the negative side; that is, by ridding ourselves of these things and others like them, we are living a good life. We are putting on a breastplate of righteousness. Another side to the same coin can be found in 1 Peter 4: 8 "Above all, love each other deeply, because love covers over a multitude of sins." By expressing our love for one another we maintain a focus which keeps the darkness pushed back and enables our "good life" to shine before men. Paul also emphasizes the importance of love as does John. Righteousness cannot be truly attained without the actual practice of love, yet true love is impossible without God. 1 Peter 5:8-9 also provides a pertinent insight into breastplate construction.

> Be self-controlled and alert. Your enemy the devil prowls around like a roaring lion looking for someone to devour. Resist him, standing firm in the faith because you know that your brothers throughout the world are undergoing the same kind of sufferings.

Every warrior knows the roaring lion is real and often seems overwhelming; however, he can be resisted. We do not have to be struck down or devoured if we will put on the breastplate of righteousness. The key, of course, is resistance. 1 Corinthians 10:13 indicates that temptation always is accompanied by an escape route for the one who looks for it. If we will resist Satan, however, we must not only look for the escape route, but actually use it.

> No temptation has seized you except what is common to man. And God is faithful; he will not let you be tempted beyond what you can bear. But when you are tempted, he will also provide a way out so that you can stand up under it.   1 Corinthians 10:13

Breastplates are fine, as far as they go. A police officer once demonstrated the effects of firing a pistol at a bulletproof vest-- it stopped the bullet. Then he took off the vest and revealed the bruises incurred when the bullet struck the vest and the body beneath the vest. Satan's weapons can make an impact on your vital organs, even when protected by the breastplate. The damage may not be deadly, but can definitely leave some spiritual "bruising" behind. Signs of bruises on the body are easy to see; just look for the "pretty" colors. Signs of spiritual bruising are less visible, but no less painful. Some of the signs are:

- A hesitancy to trust others--especially in sharing personal concerns and a Christian witness.
- An unwillingness to try new ministries or make new friends.
- Expressed feelings of insecurity, lack of love and acceptance.

When these signs occur:

A. Give the bruise time to heal. You don't press on a bruise when it is fresh. Responding immediately when the hurt is fresh is far more likely to inflict greater hurt. There is a balance in healing when too little time taken to recuperate can slow full recovery and too much time taken can lead to fear and aversion.

B. When the healing should be complete, "get right back on that horse." Don't give in to your fears that you will be bruised again. Barna writes,

"Sometimes we are overcome by fear because we have failed in the past and dare not reach for the stars again. Sometimes we dwell on our past failures or our sense of limitation. Rather than define defeat as either repeating the same mistake or refusing to take a risk, we think of it as not reaching our goals. We then allow the fear of failure to restrict our universe of opportunities to those that are safe. By focusing on our failings, we miss out on our potential." Don't allow fear to keep you from the battle."[23]

C. Practice using your shield, talked about later, to avoid bruises in the future.

If truth is the living expression of God, then righteousness is the actual life application of godliness.

> Our memory device here will be whenever we put on a shirt, or blouse, or dress to contemplate: "Living a life above reproach."

---

[23]George Barna. The Power of Vision (Ventura, CA, Regal Books, 1992), p. 124

FEET FITTED WITH READINESS THAT COMES FROM THE GOSPEL OF PEACE.

Somehow we have become convinced as we have come through the "me" generation, that if I can just take care of *me*, get *my* act together, straighten out *my* life, then I will be able to have a successful Christian life. Churches fall prey to this mentality by saying, "We're not going to worry about outreach right now. First we're going to nurture and heal our own problems." This philosophy is a recipe for continued problems and displays a basic ignorance of Christ's mission and commission to us. This mentality is opposite of that found in God's word and is a deception of Satan himself.

In sports and war we are told that one of the best defenses is a good offense, but that is, seemingly, never applied to the Christian world. Let me say this again, we are at WAR! We are constantly engaged in a spiritual struggle for the battleground of the heart. The warrior's armor will not be able to stand without these "legs" to stand on, namely a willingness to move toward other's needs, specifically their need of Christ. God in His infinite wisdom has built this into our armor so that we will:

1. **Get our eyes off ourselves.** We can become so consumed with our own struggle that we are unable to see past the problems. My mole hills grow into mountains when I lose sight of the glory of God.

2. **See others.** We all know we need to reach out (don't we?), yet when we actually do reach out to other's needs, it gives a fresh perspective to our own situations. There is something about coming into contact with another whose needs surpass ours that places our own lives in proper perspective.

3. **Give away love**. The giving away of love is crucial to making this piece of armor "ours." It is an expression of Jesus to others' hurts.

The warrior who applies himself/herself here will experience a joy that only comes from sharing Jesus. C. Peter Wagoner, a leader in church growth, observes, "In the average evangelical church, up to ten percent of the members have been given the gift of evangelism."[24] Other research has supported this statement, so I have confidence that there are capable warriors who have been gifted in this specific area: namely the winning of the lost. However, the portion of armor we are discussing is not related to that gift. Rather, the readiness applies more nearly to a concept put forth by several and stated clearly by McIntosh and Martin:

> "Some people have the joy of being involved in more than one phase of the evangelism process, but most do not. Yet there is one aspect that all people can identify with and become involved with. This aspect is vital to any evangelistic strategy. *It is inviting* ."(italics added)[25]

While McIntosh and Martin are referring to a willingness to invite others to share in a church experience, the warrior's readiness to invite others to any part of Christ's love will strengthen his defense against Satan's attacks. Paul suggests that the warrior should always be prepared to give an account of his faith. This is not an optional part of the armor, yet I repeatedly hear warriors raise a wall at this point, saying: "I'm not good with words," or, "I'm not good with people, " etc. The issue here escapes them because they focus on what they are not, instead of what Christ, through the Holy Spirit, can empower them to be. The key here is the

---

[24]C. Peter Wagner, *How to Grow a Church* (Ventura, CA, Regal Books, 1976), p. 86

[25]McIntosh & Martin, *Finding Them, Keeping Them* (), p. 55.

readiness. How often does it cross your mind to wonder if the person you are talking to knows Christ? Do you pray daily for an opportunity to share Christ, or at the very least, to invite someone to your church's services? How ready are you?

While one might think giving away love to be a side issue, however, it's relevance cannot be overstated. It is a strong defense against Satan's attacks to watch others blossom with God's love because of your touch. Midas, as the fable goes, had everything he touched turn to gold and died from lack of food and company. The warrior will know he has this piece of armor on when everything he touches brightens because of the presence of God's love. The warrior should be developing his spiritual gifts. He should be practicing the fruit of the Spirit, for these things make the gospel of peace a natural outflow of the heart into others' lives.

> Our memory association here will be putting on footwear. Take time to pray quietly for the opportunity to invite someone to worship with you on Sunday or for the opportunity to present the Gospel. Be ready to be an expression of Jesus' love to a needy world.

SHIELD OF FAITH

The shield of faith is to be used as a first line of defense, catching the fiery darts hurled at us by demonic attack. The shield's effectiveness is affected by three things.

1. Is there a shield present?

While this might be too obvious a question, it is nonetheless a fact that no shield equals no first line of defense. It means that Satan's suggestions and temptations will strike the armor, beneath which lies the sensitive organs. It means, in effect, that one's walk with Christ may be cut short by reason of multiple impacts on the breastplate which finally pierce through to the relationship underneath. Of course there must be a certain amount of faith present, else one would not be a warrior at all; however, the shield of faith is more than that. It is a faith which declares Hebrews 7:25, "Therefore he is able to save completely those who come to God through him, because he always lives to intercede for them," to be true regardless of any and all evidence put forth to the contrary.

Many have made the decision to accept Christ without being taught of the unfailing love of God and His ever-living intercession and the freedom it provides, and so have fallen away. The abiding presence of the Holy Spirit in the life of the Warrior, in spite of his failings and goof-ups is based firmly on God's promises. There is no doubt that salvation is by faith (c.f. Ephesians 2:8,9). There is also no question that faith is necessary to the successful daily life of the warrior. Romans 1: 17 declares:

> "For in the gospel a righteousness from God is revealed, a righteousness that is by faith from the first to the last, just as it is written: 'The righteous will live by faith.'"

2. What is the size of the shield?

Those used throughout history have varied in size from the ridiculously small to the preposterously large. The most popular designs were large enough to cover the torso, yet light enough not to tire the warrior. In the spiritual realm these factors also apply.

The shield can be too "heavy" to wield for long enough to truly provide protection. In spiritual warfare this describes the exact situation which has occurred repeatedly in the church. A properly constructed shield will be built out of personal experiences and tempered by the word of God. When the tempering method becomes man's precepts instead of God's, the shield quickly becomes cumbersome with legalism or too small or thin with views and standards which are not part of the word of God. The proper weight and size is achieved when the spoken word, regardless of the source, is compared against the written and living word of God for accuracy and applied to life experiences. Too many have been weighed down with a shield of man's interpretations so heavy that they simply cannot effectively move it to block Satan's attacks. Such was the case at the time of Jesus. The religious leaders of that day had added so many interpretations to the law, the average person was unable to live up to it's standards. Such, unfortunately, is the case in many fundamental churches today.

On the other side of the coin, a vast majority have listened and accepted a gospel of liberalism which does not provide enough protection. Such a loose interpretation of God's word has allowed many churches to actually consider sins such as homosexuality as "alternate lifestyles" equally valid in God's eyes as heterosexuality. Liberalism denies the truth of the written word in favor of man's logic and personal preference. Without the right size shield, the warrior will constantly be at danger.

3. How does the warrior use the shield?

The recommended method of shield usage is to place the center of the shield over the body and in front of the expected blow. The warrior must be agile enough to move quickly when blocking fiery darts, for Satan is sly and often comes from areas that we least expect. Satan's fiery darts will invariably arise from one of five different areas in the warrior's life.

A. Physical

Here the darts may take the form of illness, disease, or defect. Unlike a physical shield which actually prevents contact, the shield of faith provides a protection in the heavenly realm. Thus, the use of the shield here would be to turn the illness, disease, or defect into an opportunity to praise and glorify God instead of bitterness, discouragement, and defeat. Those who have had to suffer long with physical problems know it is faith, or lack of it, which makes all the difference.

B. Mental/Emotional

These darts are particularly prevalent in our day and age where anxieties and stress abound. Individuals are encouraged to "find themselves," and become quite confused in the process. Although the Cold War has ended there is a clinging sense of economic doom. All of these concerns and fears are magnified by Satan and launched at the warrior. The shield takes these darts and asserts that regardless of the world, regardless of my fears, I will believe God's report, namely that He is able to keep that which I have entrusted to Him and that He is looking out for my best.

C. Financial

This is one of Satan's most used darts. It never seems as if there is enough money to go around. Several years ago we had left a position at a church due to financial cutbacks. During the interim between jobs we believed that God would provide if we would continue to be faithful in our walk and service. So we prayed together, attended church faithfully, testified of God's love, tithed on what money we received, and watched God work. Time after time God brought in money, food, and rent just at the right time. Not once did we go without, not once did we ask for help, yet God always provided. It would be well for the warrior to settle this point of faith firmly in his heart, continue to move forward, and hold onto the shield.

D. Relational.

This dart, I believe, can be one of the most deadly; deadly because we really do need each other. When Satan influences one of your friends or loved ones to say things either to you or about you that are hurtful, our first response is to retaliate in like kind. Wise is the warrior who will wield the weapon of perspective and see this as a spiritual battle and block the attack with his shield of faith. 1 Corinthians 13:6-7 reads:

> "Love does not delight in evil but rejoices with the truth. It always protects, always trusts, always loves, always perseveres."

Wielding the shield of faith declares, "I believe in you even if sometimes what is said, or done, brings pain into my life."

E. Spiritual.

These fiery darts are, perhaps, the most subtle, and often take the form of a logical and rational argument. Eve's discussion in the garden with the serpent is a perfect example.

> "Now the serpent was more crafty than any of the wild animals the Lord God had made. He said to the woman, 'Did God really say, 'You must not eat from any tree in the garden'?' The woman said to the serpent, 'We may eat from the trees in the garden, but God did say, 'You must not eat fruit from the tree that is in the middle of the garden, and you must not touch it, or you will die.'' 'You will not surely die,' answered the serpent to the woman. 'For God knows that when you eat of it your eyes will be opened, and you will be like God, knowing good and evil.' When the woman saw that the fruit of the tree was good for food and pleasing to the eye, and also desirable for gaining wisdom, she took some and ate it." Genesis 3: 1-6a.

Here God's word was twisted in a way which convinced Eve that perhaps God might have made a mistake. Such, unfortunately, was not the case. Nor is it ever the case. The warrior's use of his shield must block doubt, while at the same time allow honest inquiry into how God works in the world. Disease, famine, catastrophe, are all thrown at the warrior as darts of a harsh or unloving God, when the shield of faith determines that God is at work even through tragedy for man's best.

The shield of faith requires practice to use and it is to be expected that some darts will slip through from time to time to impact on the armor of the warrior. Wielding the weapon of perseverance here, the warrior will press on, becoming ever more adept at catching Satan's fiery darts from each of these five areas.

For the memory device for the shield of faith, let's take time while putting on our pants to reaffirm our faith in a God who has our best interests at heart. Again, the three points to consider in our meditations are:

- Is there a shield present?

- What size should the shield be?

- How does the warrior use the shield?

Before moving on from this topic I want to mention the corporate nature of the shield of faith from an analogy. Ancient warriors developed a tactic when using shields as part of an army that allowed them greater defensive ability than would be possible for a single individual. By standing side by side and overlapping their shields to the front while the second row held their shields overhead in the same overlapping, they could effectively advance in spite of heavy attacks of spears or arrows.

This tactic required a lot of practice to be able to get into the proper position and to STAY in that position while moving forward, backward or turning. Making the analogy, congregations which place an emphasis upon faith and the value of relationships can be more effective in defeating the enemies darts and supporting others who are being attacked. This is no small thing and one of the great assets of becoming part of a local congregation.

THE HELMET OF SALVATION

Willard Taylor notes the helmet is,

"The symbolization of the protection which participation in God's salvation assures. If a soldier goes into the fray estranged from God, a foreigner and alien, without God, he has no guarantee of protection. But if he has been, and is, a partaker of the grace of God unto salvation, he will be 'more than conqueror.'"[26]

There is no spiritual warfare without this part of the armor. It would be like the tale of the Emperor's New Clothes. You might pretend you were walking forward in Christ, but without the helmet you would effectively be fooling only yourself. It would be like trying to run through a rain storm without getting wet. It is not possible without the proper attire of umbrella, rain coat, and boots. Thus, it is not possible to be a spiritual warrior without the salvation which comes through Christ's sacrifice.

However, with the helmet comes such assurances as these from God's word:

Romans 8:31 "if God be for us, who can be against us?'

Matthew 28: 20b "I am with you always, to the very end of the age."

---

[26]Willard H. Taylor. "Ephesians," A.F. Harper, ed., *Beacon Bible Commentary, Volume 9* (Kansas City, Beacon Hill Press, 1965), p. 265

Hebrews 6:19 "We have this hope as an anchor for the soul."

1 Thessalonians 5:9-10 "...receive salvation through our Lord Jesus Christ. He died for us so that whether we are awake or asleep, we may live together with him."

1 Thessalonians 5:24 "The one who calls you is faithful and he will do it."

2 Corinthians 1:21-22 "Now it is God who makes both us and you stand firm in Christ. He anointed us, set his seal of ownership upon us and put his Spirit in our hearts as a deposit guaranteeing what is to come."

The head is one of Satan's attack points. He is especially adept at attempting to persuade the warrior that his salvation is not complete or doesn't exist at all! Remember to seat the helmet firmly on the head, buckle the strap, and raise that shield. Do not allow Satan to call your salvation into question.

Helmets were also used with an insignia to identify to which army the soldier belonged. In the same way a proudly worn "helmet of salvation," declares with pride whose side the warrior is fighting for. The helmet of salvation becomes synonymous with Christ and His promises.

Warning: It is important to note that scriptures such as Colossians 1:23, "If you continue in your faith..." and 1 Corinthians 15:2 "...you are saved, if you hold firmly to the word," as well as life experiences, indicate that the warrior may actually be persuaded to remove his helmet, turn his back on his salvation and walk back into a life of sin. **This does not need to happen.** Have confidence in your armor and your shield.

The memory device here will be to program your minds to reflect or meditate on the fact that you are a child of the King, saved by grace while fixing your hair each day.

THE SWORD OF THE SPIRIT

The mastery of this piece of armor will prove decisive in the defensive stance of the warrior. With a carefully wielded sword, Satan's attacks can be turned before they even reach the shield. An excellent example of the use of the sword is found in Matthew *4:3-5:*

> "The tempter came to Him and said, 'If you are the son of God, tell these stones to become bread.' Jesus answered, 'It is written: man does not live on bread alone, but on every word that comes from the mouth of God.'"

Here Jesus turns Satan's attack away by use of His knowledge of the word. The truth and power of the word deny Satan any influence and block his attempt at temptation.

Other scripture points to similar usage. In fact, Psalms 119:11 reads, "I have hidden your word in my heart that I might not sin against you," and Psalm *119:105* cites, "Your word is a lamp unto my feet and a light unto my path." Both verses point to the value of the word in protecting our relationship with Jesus. For this to happen, however, it requires serious "practice" with this part of the armor. A daily exercise in Bible reading is the most basic of workouts. One method that has proven effective at this basic level is to start at a fixed point (e.g. Matthew 1:1), and read chapter one each day for a week before moving on to chapter two the next week. This allows the scripture time to actually percolate through our perceptions and conceptions. Of course, the warrior will also be reading one or more chapters daily from another part of the word in addition to this exercise.

Now add to this basic workout at least a weekly exercise in tracking down a theme (e.g. covenant, sacrifice, forgiveness, sword, etc.) through the word. Make notes and actually write out the texts. Draw parallels and arrange the texts to bring to light a clearer understanding of the theme. Themes won't have to be agonized over, they will result naturally from the other reading being done by the warrior, or by life experiences. Participation in a group Bible Study is also an appropriate exercise for the warrior as it strengthens not only his awareness of the word but provides different points of view.

Memorization of scripture is extremely helpful to the warrior. While not everyone may be able to take full advantage of this practice, it has proven to be of significant help in actual combat against the enemy. Remember the experience of Jesus as He was being tempted, cited above. It was His recitation of the Word which blocked the temptation. In a similar vein, memorization and application actually form the sword. Whatever the method of memorization of the word, such as memorizing scripture by memorizing scripture choruses, such memorization will give the warrior power to block Satan's attacks before they even strike the shield.

The word may also be used in ways other than in turning away attack. Hebrews 4:12 helps us to understand another use for this part of the armor.

> "For the word of God is living and active. Sharper than any double--edged sword, it penetrates even to dividing soul and spirit, joints and marrow; it judges the thoughts and attitudes of the heart."

The sword is also useful in helping to cut away the unnecessary and defective portions of our lives. It's kind of like pruning. Pruning is a process whereby the parts of a tree or plant that do not produce fruit or add to the beauty, are cut off. The word of God reveals in us, through our reading and listening to the proclamation of the word, parts of our natural attitudes which must be eliminated for our own good. Jeremiah 23:29 shares the sense of this pruning: "'Is not my word like a fire,' declares the Lord, 'and like a hammer that breaks a rock in pieces.'" Sometimes the word applied to our own lives seems like a fire and even here Satan may flash the temptation to quit. Remember, though, that the pruning of whatever attitude or behavior will work to the warrior's best interest if he will have confidence in the One who prunes. After all, it is Jesus who is the Living Word and He only corrects those He loves. Wise is the warrior who will accept the word as his lamp and guide, listening to what it says not only about the war, but about his own life as well. James 1:22 emphasizes an important part of this process, "Do not merely listen to the word, and so deceive yourselves. Do what it says." The temptation will be to intellectualize the scripture without making a life application;   to rationalize my behavior in spite of the admonition of the word. Doing so merely "deceives" yourself. Make the word a change agent for your life.

Your memory device for the sword will be your keys, or whatever it is you keep in your pocket or purse that you use often. Think about your Bible, a special text, or verse every time you touch that item.

Questions:

1. How is an understanding of the helmet of salvation important to ongoing effectiveness?

2. What factors influence the size and thickness of your shield?

3. How can the sword be used to protect the shield and the rest of the armor.

4. Why do good Christians have to endure temptations?

5. What temptations is the armor effective against?

6. Why is the constant presence of the armor necessary?

CHAPTER 6
SPIRITUAL AUTHORITY

The issue of authority is one which finds its roots when Adam and Eve questioned God's authority by violating his command to not eat of the fruit of the tree of knowledge. It is the core reason why Adam and Eve fell and were expelled from the garden. It is the core of all of man's problems to this day; in essence the elevation of "self" above any other authority or power. By another name it is called the carnal nature. Relinquishing authority is the intent of sanctification; by fully submitting to God and consecrating ourselves totally to him can we come into a state similar to that enjoyed by Adam and Eve before the fall. Only a clear understanding of authority will allow the warrior to grow in his relationship with Christ and in his ability to overcome the evil one.

When the 72 returned from their evangelistic efforts, Jesus said,

"I have given you authority to trample on snakes and scorpions and to overcome all the power of the enemy; nothing will harm you. However, do not rejoice that the spirits submit to you, but rejoice that your names are written in heaven."(Luke 10:19-20)

The 72 rejoiced at their authority over the powers of this world, only to be reminded by Jesus where to place their true joy. There is no doubt that authority is a part of the warrior's equipment to overcome the enemy, yet there is also little doubt that the *misplacement* of authority has destroyed many warriors who either did not understand its proper use or placed their joy in its use instead of the source of the authority.

Robert Kelley in *The Power of Followership*, defines five different styles of following, or submitting to authority, which, I believe, accurately apply to the warrior and his understanding of authority.[27] Those five styles of followership are:

Passive - uninformed and unmotivated with little desire to be informed and/or motivated.

Conformist - the yes man. He may be informed and motivated but is too fearful of failure to initiate any ministries or take initiative on his own. Sought out by many leaders because of a fear of conflict, the conformist is usually a timid and fearful warrior who would more likely hide his talent for fear of the consequences if he used it wrongly.

Pragmatist - informed but not very motivated. The pragmatist does mediocre work and avoids anything with the risk of failure. As a spiritual warrior, his primary question is: "How little do I have to do and still make it to heaven?"

Alienated - informed, motivated, and self-starting, with only one problem. Somewhere along the way the alienated follower felt he was betrayed, or a trust was broken, and now all his energies are directed toward critical input which is divisive and usually abrasive.

Exemplary - informed, motivated, competent, willing to learn, and a self-starter. As a spiritual warrior the exemplary follower is capable of dreaming the dream and making his part of the dream an asset to the overall vision.

Each of these follower styles may be found in the church and in the pages of the Bible. While much space could be given to a thorough break-

---

[27]Robert E. Kelley, *The Power of Followership* (Doubleday Currency, 1992)

down of each style, it is the exemplary follower who most nearly describes the true spiritual warrior. Different examples from the Bible might include Abraham, Moses, Noah, David, Peter, Paul, etc.; yet, the greatest example of the exemplary follower is our leader, Jesus Christ. The next few pages will be given to examining His example and what we might be able to learn from that example.

Jesus was under authority.

The following passages indicate Jesus' awareness that He was in submission to a higher authority.

John 5:30 "By myself I can do nothing; I judge only as I hear, and my judgment is just, for I seek not to please myself but him who sent me."

John 6:38 "For I have come down from heaven not to do my will but to do the will of him who sent me."

John 7:16 "Jesus answered, 'My teaching is not my own. It comes from him who sent me.'"

John 7:28 "'...Yes you know me, and you know where I am from. I am not here on my own, but he who sent me is true.'"

John 8:42 "Jesus said to them, "If God were your Father, you would love me, for I came from God and now am here. I have not come on my own; but he sent me."

Jesus lived a life of submission to the one who had sent Him into the world. He was completely submissive to the will of the Father, even while being tempted by Satan in the wilderness. Murray writes,

"Christ found this life of entire self-renunciation, of absolute submission and dependence upon the Father's will, to be one of perfect peace and joy. He lost nothing by giving everything to God."[28]

---

[28]Andrew Murray, *Humility*, (Whitaker House, 1982), 23

When we see Jesus in this context we better understand the part He played in God's grand plan for our salvation. Jesus is an exemplary follower because he has committed himself to the Father's plan. Kelley states that to be an exemplary follower, "First, identify what you most want to commit yourself to."[29] Jesus repeatedly directed attention to the Father and went about fulfilling the Father's plan with a single-minded devotion.

A further example of His initiative in fulfilling the Father's plan may be seen in his ministry between the wedding in Cana and the resurrection. The plan required that Jesus would be the perfect sacrifice which would purchase salvation. A passive follower would never have committed to that. The conformist follower probably wouldn't have made it past the temptations in the desert. The pragmatic followers may have shared the teachings, miracles, and healings but not likely the death. The alienated follower, even if accepting the assignment, would have been negative and disparaging up to the end and would have balked at the final step. Jesus' example, however, is of one who invests himself in teachings, miracles, and healings up to the last moment. He went beyond what was required to add extra benefit to His sacrifice, even though that extra benefit took more effort and perhaps even hastened the crucifixion.

Jesus was under God's authority, and he submitted to that authority fully, freely and without hesitation. By doing so, he left a clear pattern for us to follow as we follow Him.

---

[29]Kelley, p. 133.

Jesus was in Authority

By understanding to whom He was in submission, Jesus also stood in authority over all things. "All things have been committed to me by my Father." (Matthew 11:27a) Jesus was in subjection to God, while being in authority over all things. Being in subjection to authority while at the same time being in authority is not unique; In fact, it is the very nature of what authority means. Webster defines authority as: "the power or right to give commands, take action, etc."[30] Like all power, the nature of authority is revealed when the source of the authority is discovered. In the case of Jesus, that source was God.

Indeed, as Nee observes,

"The controversy of the universe is centered on who shall have the authority, and our conflict with Satan is the direct result of our attributing authority to God."[31]

Jesus exercised his God-given authority by commanding demons to come out of people--by bringing the weather under control--by healing diseases--by teaching. Yet, although he had the authority, he refrained from calling down angels to deliver him from the cross or otherwise damage the fulfillment of the plan. His authority extended to every part of life, yet, instead of making things easier on himself, he repeatedly used that authority to bring God to the people in a tangible way. Dauntless, he spoke words of authority to demons, expecting their complete fulfillment. He knew where his authority came from and he knew he was in authority.

---

[30]Webster's New World Dictionary, (The World Publishing Company, 1958, 59), 12

[31]Watchman Nee, Spiritual Authority, (Christian Fellowship Publishers, New Your, 1972), 12

The Warrior Under Authority

The warrior, before he can exercise authority, must truly understand what it means to be under authority. "...Obedience to authority is the first lesson a worker ought to learn...." writes Nee.[32] If you respond that you are ready to place yourself in full subjection to Jesus Christ, let me ask: are you currently walking in all the light He has shown you? Does your inner spirit stand before God clear of rebellion or deceit? Can you see evidence of passive, conformist, pragmatic or even alienated followership styles in your life? Jesus spoke much of the relationship of our attention to money and authority. Are you a faithful steward of the resources God has entrusted into your care? Do you tithe to your local storehouse, the church where you attend and serve? Do you give additional offerings of love to the church and others as directed by the Holy Spirit? This issue of money is an accurate thermometer for most of how ready they are to submit to authority. Contentiousness here is a sure sign of unresolved issues of ownership and submission. To submit to God means to submit to One who loves you and wants the best for your life as seen from a heavenly perspective. Without submission from the heart, we are deceiving ourselves. When my sons were young they liked to play ninja. They loved to kick and chop and twirl around. To them it was almost real, yet they wanted nothing to do with the disciplines that would make real their pretend skills. Where are you at in your life? Are you ready to follow the pattern of Jesus and become an exemplary follower? If you are ready to fully submit to God, though the road to that submission is often hard and rocky, be assured that you have chosen the only road to becoming a successful warrior.

---

[32]Nee, p. 23

The warrior can test himself on this point in two ways. *First*, in his daily consideration of God's word. By now the warrior should have learned that the proper use of the sword depends upon three things: its sharpness, the skill and the strength of the one wielding the sword. In the same way, the benefit of the word comes through three things: reading, understanding, and applying the truths of scripture to our lives. The Word is the tangible presence of the living God. No warrior can be an exemplary follower unless he submits to the authority of the Word. Are you obedient to the word of God in every particular as God reveals these truths to you? It does no good to try to argue why this or that should not apply. Much wiser is the warrior who accepts his training and responds immediately, in God's strength, to what he has been shown. Jesus said, "If you love me, you will obey what I command." (John 14:15).

Second, are you willing to submit to those whom God has placed in authority?

> "Everyone must submit himself to the governing authorities, for there is no authority except that which God has established. The authorities that exist have been established by God. Consequently, he who rebels against the authority is rebelling against what God has instituted, and those who do so will bring judgment on themselves. For rulers hold no terror for those who do right, but for those who do wrong. Do you want to be free from fear of the one in authority? Then do what is right and he will commend you. For he is God's servant to do you good. But if you do wrong, be afraid, for he does not bear the sword for nothing. He is God's servant, an agent of wrath to bring punishment on the wrongdoer. Therefore it is necessary to submit to the authorities, not only because of possible punishment but also because of conscience..." Romans 13:1-5

For many, acknowledging human authority is the most difficult step of all. "I don't mind being subject to God," we say, "but I don't have to listen to that Pastor." Yet, if indeed "that Pastor" is speaking according to the Spirit of God, as verified by scripture, and has been placed in a position of authority, then we must obey, or walk out of the will of God. Subjection to appointed authority is quite often the dividing line separating true warriors from those who merely wish to play at a game. Scripture indicates that God appoints leaders who must give an account of their leadership. Exemplary followership applies to how they fulfill their duties as well as to the warrior under their authority. While we are accountable for our own actions, we are also interconnected in a framework of authority. The text cited from Romans speaks clearly to the responsibility of the warrior to governmental leaders, yet scripture is also clear about following individuals placed in spiritual authority.

> 1 Corinthians 16: 15,16 "You know that the household of Stephanas were the first converts in Achaia, and they have devoted themselves to the service of the saints. I urge you, brothers, *to* submit *to such as these and to everyone who joins in the work, and labors* at it." (bold italics added)

> 1 Thessalonians 5:12,13 "Now we ask you, brothers, *to respect those who work hard* among *you, who are over you in the Lord and who admonish you. Hold them in the highest regard in love because of their work.* Live in peace with each other." (bold italics added)

> 1 Timothy 5:17 *"The elders who direct the affairs of the church well are worthy of double honor, especially those whose work is preaching and teaching."*(bold italics added)

> Hebrews 13:17,*"Obey your leaders and submit to their authority. They keep watch over you as men who must give an account.* Obey them so that their work will be a joy, not a burden, for that would be of no advantage to you." (bold italics added)

Nee highlights why scripture is so clear about honoring those who are spiritual leaders:

> "...subjection to authority is not being subject to a person, but being subject to the anointing which is upon that person, the anointing which came to him when God ordained him to be an authority."[33]

---

[33]Nee, p. 43

Practically, if the warrior is unable to acknowledge God's appointed leadership which they can see and touch, how will they be able to follow God's leadership? Thus David's honoring of Saul, even when he had the chance to kill him, makes perfect sense (1 Samuel 14:4-6). No matter how bad a leader Saul became, it was God's prerogative to remove him as leader, not man's. Churches have floundered and individuals have been destroyed at this point. God's call is to obedience and submission to His wisdom, which includes not only the appointment of governments, but the appointment of spiritual leaders (e.g. pastors, teachers, etc.) as well. Until the warrior recognizes that he is under the authority, of God and His appointees as well, he will never be effective in exercising authority.

The Warrior in Authority

The spiritual warrior has more authority than is commonly used. Jesus told the seventy-two: "I have given you authority to trample on snakes and scorpions and to overcome all the power of the enemy; nothing will harm you." (Luke 10:19) Jesus is speaking here to seventy-two traveling evangelists. When they returned they exclaimed with joy, "Lord, even the demons submit to us in your name." (Luke 10:17) Mark 16:17-18 adds that authority to the New Testament Church:

> "And these signs will accompany those who believe: In my name they will drive out demons; they will speak in new tongues; they will pick up snakes with their hands; and when they drink deadly poison, it will not hurt them at all; they will place their hands on sick people, and they will get well."

In a democracy, the source of a political leader's authority would be the will of the people. In spiritual warfare the source of authority is Jesus, who, acting in submission to the Father, declares that

> "anyone who has faith in me will do what I have been doing. He will do even greater things than these because I am going to the Father. And I

will do whatever you ask in my name so that the Son may bring glory to the Father. You may ask me for anything in my name and I will do it." (John 14:12-14)

There are other areas of authority available to the warrior as he grows in his relationship with God and his use of spiritual weapons. These areas include but are not limited to:

- Healing (physical, mental, and emotional)
- Attitudes
- Weather and other forces of nature
- Miracles

I have one final word to add on spiritual authority. Jesus indicated to the 72, "do not rejoice that the spirits submit to you, but rejoice that your names are written in heaven." (Luke 10:20) Exercising spiritual authority without an appropriate spirit of humility can be disastrous.

Questions

1. How did Adam and Eve defy God's authority? Discuss why God placed them in authority over the earth.

2. How did Jesus demonstrate that he was in submission to God? Why was his submission important?

3. Why is understanding our subjection to governmental and spiritual leaders important in assuming authority?

4. Can an individual who will not submit to God's appointed authority be able to fully exercise spiritual authority himself?

5. Discuss what being in authority and taking authority means to you.

6. What style of followership best describes your response at work, at home, at church, in the community, etc.?

7. Assuming that the exemplary follower best describes the Spiritual Warrior, what actions do you need to take to become an exemplary follower?

CHAPTER 7
SATAN'S WEAPONS AND STRATEGIES

Any look at the principles of Spiritual Warfare would be incomplete without at least an overview of the enemy's capabilities. Although Satan is first mentioned in Genesis when he entices Adam and Eve, we see his place much earlier in history by looking at Revelation 12:7-10:

> "And there was war in heaven. Michael and his angels fought the dragon, and the dragon and his angels fought back. But he was not strong enough, and they lost their place in heaven. The great dragon was hurled down-- that ancient serpent called the devil, or Satan, who leads the whole world astray. He was hurled to the earth, and his angels with him. Then I heard a loud voice in heaven say: 'Now have come the salvation and the power and the kingdom of our God, and the authority of his Christ. For the accuser of our brothers, who accuses them before our God day and night has been hurled down.'"

Satan, the ringleader of a failed coup, and his followers, were hurled out of heaven to the earth. As was stated in chapter one, Satan's basic goal is to divert glory from the Son of God and so, perhaps, manipulate another, more successful coup. While this is impossible (Satan has already been condemned and is even now awaiting his eternal punishment) Satan is working toward his goal with all his resources. His basic strategy is twofold:

1.   Keep non-believers from finding out about salvation.

2.   Subvert believers away from their faith in Christ.

Warner writes,

"There is a sense in which all spiritual warfare is a matter of spiritual effectiveness or ineffectiveness. At the root of this matter is the maturity level of our personal and corporate Christian lives. It is imperative that we be aware of the tactics Satan uses to disrupt our lives in this area."[34]

It is important to note at the onset that all of Satan's weapons are built on the same framework. That framework is described in John 8:44:

> "You belong to your father, the devil, and you want to carry out your father's desire. He was a murderer from the beginning, not holding to the truth, for there is no truth in him. When he lies, he speaks his native language, for he is a liar and the father of lies."

He is the father of lies and those lies are at the heart of each of the weapons described in this chapter. His goal is the destruction of your soul and his attacks range from the subtle to the violent. As you read through this list of Satanic weapons, envision how Satan might use each one against you and so begin to prepare yourself for his attack.

DOUBT

One of the chronic problems of our day is self-image. Fostered by the insecurity of the 60's, and the following generations, many are experiencing an uncertainty about "who they are" and where they "fit in." This in turn evidences itself in many ways including increased suicide rate, obesity, health issues, and poor work ethic, not to mention a lack of pride in the quality of work produced. While it might be more accepted to lay this problem at the feet of Dr. Spock and the legacy of the sixties, or just blame our parents, the true, underlying cause, when seen from the perspective of spiritual warfare, is demonic. Demonic influences in the television, newspapers, advertising, schools, and governments have led to a basic mistrust of almost everyone and everything, including, and perhaps

---

[34]Warner, p. 97

most especially, ourselves. Recent presidential elections are a prime example of this lack of trust. The average response of the voters before the election elicits such comments as, "Well, I'm going to vote for (insert name of candidate here), but I don't think any of them are just what this country needs right now." Even our most trusted officials are perceived with suspicion and doubt.

Satan plays upon this doubt and focuses it on those in the prison mode. These individuals, without an active relationship with Jesus, are kept from hearing about God's saving grace at all. If they do learn about Jesus' love and the possibility of a relationship with God, they are persuaded to doubt that there is any truth to the claims of Christianity. Every possible effort is put forth by the demonic forces to malign the Christian faith and portray it as weak and ineffectual. Instead, other non-saving philosophies are put forth as viable (e.g. both cults and occults). Through use of lies, Satan's minions increase an overall spirit of doubt that clouds reality like a fog bank conceals the road.

For those who manage to claim Christ, the weapon of doubt is still effective, perhaps even more than before. Satan's emphasis is still upon Christianity's supposed inability to assist the warrior in being victorious. Satan attempts to trick the warrior into believing there is a connection between life trauma and faith. His demons whisper, "If you really had faith, you wouldn't be experiencing these problems, you sure don't have much faith," or, "How could God possibly love someone like you." "You are never going to measure up to His standards, you might as well quit." The seeds of doubt are already in place and, unless eradicated, will sprout and eventually overwhelm the warrior. For example, one person, although very capable and desirous of spiritual growth, is continually plagued by doubts of his own worthiness. Another, when faced with difficulties, begins to doubt that God truly cares about his specific situations. In both cases the temptation is to believe the lies and draw back from fellowship with God and the church. On the surface this "drawback" is explained, "So that I can get a little perspective on my problems." Realistically it is an opportunity for Satan to attack even harder and drive an even deeper wedge between the individual and God. Although difficult, it is imperative that the warrior experiencing doubt not separate himself from worship or Christian fellowship. The weapon of praise, particularly in a congregational setting, is powerful against Satan's weapon of doubt.

Similarly, contact with Christian friends can help dispel doubt. The choosing of one's friends wisely *cannot be overstated*. Too many times our choice of friends does little more than mire us down in negatives and gloom because they themselves are not victorious in their walk with God. Then there are the "friends" who feel compelled to judge others instead of being a support. As a friend, the warrior must be genuine while expressing a positive attitude. He should avoid being a "Job's comforter" who focuses the problem away from it's true source and discourages the warrior.

Doubt may also be deeply ingrained enough in the personality of the warrior that it is actually a demonic stronghold. If this is true, then the strategy described in Chapter 8 will assist the warrior in demolishing that stronghold.

> **Questions**:
>
> 1. Discuss the sources of doubt which affect your life as they relate to God's activity in you life.
> 2. Friends have a powerful effect upon our perception and can be a help or hindrance in our Christian walk. Why is this so? Have you had negative experiences?

DISEASE

By disease, I mean any condition of ill health which lessens the body's ability to function. Of course much time could be spent here describing just what it means to function and how physical and mental distress for one person do not necessarily mean the same for another. Important as this is in a discussion for a group, individually, I think each one knows when his body is not performing up to "par." Thus, whether it be a cold, physical or mental handicap, cancer, migraine, or even a pulled muscle, there is a definite lessening of the warrior's energies. Disease in these terms, plays upon doubt, bringing to bear all that goes with that weapon, but carries it's own weight in destructive powers. Let me state here that not all diseases are started by demonic forces. There is too great a myth already of Satan's power and I want to discourage seeing him as all powerful--he is not. Because of the fall and the genetic problems since then, there is plenty of pain and disease already existent. Satan has little need to manufacture more disease and disabilities although he still does do so for specific individuals under attack. He does, however, use whatever diseases and disabilities already present in insidious ways to accomplish his goals.

Disease has the ability to draw all of our focus into symptom relief. It has the power to redirect all of our physical and mental energies toward coping with its affect upon our bodies. For many the pain can be so intense as to block all rational thought. For others, the on-goingness of the disease begins to break down all reserves of strength until there seems to be no point to life. The non-believer in these scenarios has not the strength or the will to consider salvation. The warrior, too, is unable to focus on issues of salvation. The difference here is that one has already made the choice for Jesus, and regardless of "feelings" and pain, the assurance of an eternal destiny in heaven is guaranteed.

Disease, particularly the long-term kind, is used by Satan in conjunction with another weapon, despair, to bring about apathy toward God in the life of the warrior, leading to separation and reinstatement in Satan's prison. God does provide healing, as will be discussed later; however, *the main issue in combating disease as a weapon is not divine healing but the warrior's perseverance*. The warrior who takes seriously the promises of God and has faith in Him, no matter the physical effects of the body, will stand firm in his faith. Probably the best illustration of this point is found in Daniel 3. Here three of Daniel's friends were confronted with the choice to serve God or turn away from their faith and thereby save themselves physical pain. Their response is classic and vital for the warrior, particularly when confronted with the weapon of disease.

> "Shadrach, Meshach and Abednego replied to the king, '0 Nebuchadnezzar, we do not need to defend ourselves before you in this matter. If we are thrown into the blazing furnace, the God we serve is able to save us from it, and he will rescue us from your hand, 0 king. But even if he does not, we want you to know 0 king, that we will not serve your gods or worship the image of gold you have set up." (Daniel 3:16-18)

Satan's use of disease has been accorded far too much power in the minds and lives of warriors. It has been puffed up in its importance until the mere word of some forms of disease (e.g. cancer) strikes fear and desperation into otherwise stalwart warriors.

Disease, as Satan's weapon, does have one weakness. Because it tangibly affects the body, the power of God, when wielded in faith can be visibly manifested in powerful ways. This can happen in two ways. The first is the warrior who, in spite of the disease, exhibits the love of Christ in service to others. The second is when God chooses to heal, the testimony of the warrior is greater than before and his weapon of perseverance is enhanced. Keep in mind, , *the main issue in combating disease as a weapon is not divine healing but the warrior's perseverance*. Getting sidetracked into a focus on healing and/or the lack thereof is another of Satan's weapons. Disease can open a door of opportunity for the gospel to be presented to the non-believer, either because of faithfulness in the midst of the disease or because of healing, which can be much more effective due to the RQ[35] discussed in chapter two. This weapon of Satan's has no power to touch the soul, regardless of his lies and wise is the warrior who has his resolve firmly in place, ready at all times for the cunning attacks of the enemy.

Questions:

1. Disease or any ill health is problematic for many Christians who assume it to evidence of a lack of faith, yet these same Christians also go through bouts of flu or colds, if not worse, themselves. It is a fact that everyone dies eventually. Describe how Satan has used this weapon to undermine the faith of someone you know.
2. Discuss the response of Christians to the presence of sickness within the church.
3. How you personally understand the role of faith related to long-term illness vs short-term illness – is there a difference? Why or why not?

DEBT

When the issue of money is discussed there seems to well up within the soul a defensiveness about why and how money is used. 1 Timothy 6:10 suggests that the root of all kinds of evil is the love of money.

---

[35] Readiness Quotient (RQ) is discussed more fully on page 12 of this book.

Jesus says in Matthew 6:24, speaking of masters, that, "You cannot serve both God and money." His clear pronouncement here is that the love of money may assume the position of master of the soul, above all other considerations. As a weapon, Satan employs our natural concern for our well being and financial security in two distinct ways.

1. There is never enough

> Matthew 6:19 describes where we are not to lay up our treasurers."Do not store up for yourselves treasures on earth, where moth and rust destroy, and where thieves break in and steal."

Jesus' parable in Luke 12:13-21 tells of one whose life is consumed by the greed for more and more and more.

> "Someone in the crowd said to him, 'Teacher, tell my brother to divide the inheritance with me.' Jesus replied, 'Man, who appointed me a judge or an arbiter between you?' Then he said to them, 'Watch out! Be on your guard against all kinds of greed; a man's life does not consist in the abundance of his possessions.' And he told them this parable: 'The ground of a certain rich man produced a good crop. He thought to himself, 'What shall I do? I have no place to store my crops.' Then he said, 'This is what I'll do. I will tear down my barns and build bigger ones, and there I will store all my grain and my goods. And I'll say to myself, 'You have plenty of good things laid up for many years. Take life easy; eat, drink and be merry." But God said to him, 'You fool! This very night your life will be demanded from you. Then who will get what you have prepared for yourself?' This is how it will be with anyone who stores up things for himself but is not rich toward God."

Satan uses the weapon of debt to instill in us a desire for a lifestyle just out of our reach. When this happens the temptation is to despair and cast God in the role of a "gimme god" whose main role is to give me the style of life which I think I deserve. Our attitude easily shifts away from the relationship which we have with Jesus through faith, to the "needs" (really "wants") we have. Let me say here that there are valid "needs." There are basic needs which we all have which are clearly addressable in the context of God's word and we are promised by God that He will supply those needs.

Even here Satan can twist these valid needs to such a perspective that we forget our warfare does not use the weapons of this world. The misled and ill-trained warrior often begins to attack the need with weapons that are outside of God's will. *Any financial dealings which lack complete integrity toward God and others will become a barrier to an effective walk with God.* The weapons of spiritual warfare are not the weapons of this world. If you doubt this happens, look carefully at the lesson in Acts 5 of Ananias and Sapphira. This couple's sin and downfall was not that they kept a portion of the money received from a land sale, rather it was their use of an inappropriate weapon, deception, to protect their own welfare. Satan won a victory in their souls because they put the love of money ahead of their desire to walk in the ways of God.

Unfortunately the plight of Ananias and Sapphira is all too common. Either we are possessed of money enough to meet our needs or we do not have enough to cover the basic expenses. In either case, Satan's strategy is to get the warrior to focus on himself and his own well being ahead of his relationship with God. His tactic in debt is to distort and twist legitimate doctor's bills, broken appliances, utilities, rent, etc. into a nightmare, all clamoring for attention and all demanding priority. Having bills is not wrong, nor, in fact, is being in debt. While Hamlet is advised to neither borrow nor lend, scripture indicates that the Year of Jubilee was to be a year when all debts would be forgiven, thus indicating that borrowing and lending was a normal part of everyday life. Today, however, many have abused borrowing against tomorrow as a license to live far above their income and thereby place money and its acquisition in a position of power in their lives. They have become by necessity, a lover of money, or if not money, the things which money can buy, and thereby allow an influx of evils into their lives.

> "A strong sense of hopelessness.... That is the way many Christians describe their inner feelings about their finances. They feel as if they are aimlessly adrift in an endless stream of borrowing. Unpaid bills occupy more and more of their thoughts. They honestly believe there is no way out of their debt dilemma."[36]

While debt is overwhelming, there is hope. There are strategies which will help you get a handle on where your money is going and how to reduce your debt load to manageable levels and even eliminate it altogether. One such workbook is The Victory Book, by John Avanzini and Patrick Ondrey. In The Victory Book, you are led by use of scripture and experience through steps which will liberate you from the crushing burden of debt.

Satan's weapon of debt is harmless against the warrior who recognizes his resources and lives within those resources, trusting God to make up the difference. The warrior who sees money not as a god but, quite simply, as controlled by the hand and will of God, will be a diligent worker, yet one who doesn't place work and overtime ahead of his relationship with Christ or his family.

2. My Tithe

Even after one is born into the kingdom of God and becomes a warrior, Satan is able to subvert many by use of this weapon. In Malachi 3:8-11 we find:

> "Will a man rob God? Yet you rob me. But you ask, 'How do we rob you?' In tithes and offerings. You are under a curse--the whole nation of you--

---

[36]John Avanzini, *War on Debt: Breaking the Power of Debt* (His Image Ministries, 1990), 11

because you are robbing me. Bring the whole tithe into the storehouse, that there may be food in my house. 'Test me in this,' says the Lord Almighty, 'and see if I will not throw open the floodgates of heaven and pour out so much blessing that you will not have room enough for it. I will prevent pests from devouring your crops, and the vines in your fields will not cast their fruit.' says the Lord Almighty."

There are several things which must be defined before we proceed:

- Tithe --as listed in the law of Moses is a tenth of our increase.

- Storehouse--defined in our day as the local congregation where you attend

- Offerings--financial or other gifts above and beyond the tithe, given solely as an expression of love or appreciation. Looking at the Malachi passage, several things come to light which apply to this weapon in the hands of Satan.

First: The warrior who does not give his tithe is stealing from God. Theft is, as we know, a sin. The one who does not tithe is a sinner, regardless of what he professes with his tongue (1 John 3:8) and the wages of sin is death (Romans 6:23). This is not a popular thought, but it is clearly the reverse side of what happens to many. If I believe I don't have enough, I simply don't give my tithes and offerings to God. Too many Christians wonder why God is not blessing in their lives or why they do not have a deeper sense of God, while ignoring His word concerning their tithe. The curse recounted in Malachi is not just an Old Testament standard. It is impossible to walk forward in our relationship with Jesus if there is any confusion about the proper place of money, and the only way to adequately demonstrate our awareness is to be faithful in our tithes and offerings. John Maxwell, author and President of Enjoy Ministries, tells of a board member who was displeased with some of the changes that Pastor Maxwell seemed to be leading the church in and approached the Pastor one day and told him he was going to stop his tithe. John's reply was, "Well if that's how you feel you should tell the right person." Somewhat perplexed but willing the board member asked who that would be. John replied, "God, let's just kneel right here and pray, 'Dear God, here is your servant and he has just decided in his heart that he is going to begin robbing from you by not paying his tithe." Just about that time, the board member not liking the sound of the prayer stopped and said, 'Wait a minute, I didn't say I was going to rob God." John's response pointed to the clear reference in the Bible about where the tithe truly goes and who it belongs to. After this there was no more talk of withholding tithe. If you doubt this, check the Book.

Second: Malachi 3:10 is the only reference of which I am aware which challenges us to put God to the test. On paper it does not make sense for anyone to give 10% of their income to the God's work. From a secular viewpoint, there doesn't seem to be any way that the "ends," which were just barely meeting before, will meet at all now. To the world such a practice as tithing is ridiculous. God, however, says "test me." Interestingly, remember, this is the same God who created the stars, the earth, and all who walk upon it. God challenges us to test Him, not just as an occasional thing, but as a lifestyle; make tithing and offerings a part of our lives and see what happens. I cannot record here the many testimonials of those who have so "tested" God. From the very wealthy to the most poor, the testimonies come back again and again of God's faithfulness to make the 90% go farther that the 100% did before. God passes the test of providing in abundance to meet personal needs and other blessings.

Satan does not want the warrior to take this challenge. He does not mind if you throw $5 or even $20 in the offering plate once in a while, after all, it eases the conscience and pushes back the sense of "I'm not doing something I should be doing." Satan does not want the warrior to experience the abundant blessings promised. As a side benefit, if Satan can keep warriors from tithing and divert their tithes to other "needs," he can keep the local congregation short of the funds it needs to make an impact upon the local community where it is located. He can keep the church leaders focused on money needs instead of lost souls. Too many of our churches have become bogged down by this strategy of the Devil.

Debt is a powerful weapon of Satan, yet a subtle one. The abuse of monies given in good faith to certain television evangelists has furthered Satan's work in this regard and undermined the faith of many. Satan has only to suggest misappropriation of funds and tithes and offerings wither up and die. The true warrior will hold fast to the teachings of the word, however, and trust God to handle His church and the actual expenditures. He will be faithful in giving.

Questions:

1. How has debt affected your charitable giving?
2. Do you tithe? If not, what is your rationale and how does it fit with scripture?
3. Have you experienced the blessings of Malachi 3:10? If so, describe.

DESPAIR

The fourth weapon in Satan's arsenal of deception is despair. There are some who seem to suggest that Christians are always happy and full of joy; that, somehow they are impervious to the trials of life which arise. While our attitudes are largely controllable and much is being written lately about taking charge of our attitudes, as humans, even as redeemed humans, we experience the reality of despair upon occasion. David, God's favorite, experienced times of despair,

> Psalm 77:1-9 records some of his thoughts at such a time.
>
> "I cried out to God for help; I cried out to God to hear me. When I was in distress, I sought the Lord; at night I stretched Out untiring hands and my soul refused to be comforted. I remembered you, 0 God, and I groaned; I mused, and my spirit grew faint. You kept my eyes from closing; I was too troubled to speak. I thought about the former days, the years of long ago; I remembered my songs in the night. My heart mused and my spirit inquired: 'Will the Lord reject forever? Will he never show his favor again? Has his unfailing love vanished forever? Has his promise failed for all time? Has God forgotten to be merciful? Has he in anger withheld his compassion?"'

Jesus also experienced times of sorrow and even despair. Luke 13:3 1 records his despair over the plight of Jerusalem. We read all through the gospels of his compassion, prayers, and even tears for the death of a loved friend.

Despair in times of heartache and loss, in times of weariness and pain are all natural feelings. Such feelings are not wrong nor do they make anyone less of a Christian and warrior for the kingdom. Too many times we preachers have belabored our flocks for valid feelings in the midst of their personal traumas. Too many times warriors have fallen, pierced by their own comrades who seemed very willing to condemn and judge in spite of Christ's admonishments otherwise.

To be in despair is not necessarily of Satan. Despair and depression may have chemical causes as well as those arising from crisis or trauma. The difference is not easily discernable and those suffering from despair and depression often receive less compassion and support than do those dealing with the more obvious weapon of "disease." Despair and depression are not "quick fixes." The warrior who deals with this weapon personally no more wants to be discouraged or down than one might want to have cancer. Truly we need to be careful of hasty judgments and feelings of superiority when we come across others dealing with despair.

Satan's weapon of despair goes beyond, but may include, feelings which arise due to the circumstances of life or chemical imbalances to become a lifestyle of hopelessness and negativism. Despair is typically the result of one of four causes:

1. Circumstantial despair. Circumstantial despair is caused by the traumas of life which are most often unexpected and have profound influence on our lives. Death, disaster, war, etc., all fit into this category.

2. Chemical Imbalance. Although some will deny this as a valid category, my experiences have demonstrated that there are some individuals whose body's have a chemical imbalance which requires replacement or additive chemicals in order to function smoothly. In some cases the replacement chemicals are only partially effective and may have side effects which add to an already complicated presentation.

3. Chronic despair. Chronic despair is just as devastating as a chemical imbalance, but in this case medical assistance in the form of chemicals is not as effective. I have found most chronic despair to be the result of deep emotional scarring from early in the individual's life. Although, there is victory for these individuals, it will only come as they are able to deal with the scars of their past, and usually over a fairly long period of time. Expecting them to "just pull themselves up by their bootstraps" is unrealistic and can even be destructive. Individuals who suffer from this type of despair need a network of supporting individuals who can walk with them through this long valley.

4. Spiritual laziness. The warrior who falls into this category has grown lax in the reading of the word and the weapon of prayer. He has begun to take his relationship with Christ for granted.

One way to recognize this as an attack of Satan weapon is through the conversation of the one so afflicted. The conversation is almost invariably filled with a hopelessness or even a doomsday outlook on life. The warrior so afflicted will find it hard to think about anything at all and will usually be confused about his relationship with Christ. In fact, in their confusion, many warriors cut themselves off from any contact, especially those they feel they might have let down by being in despair.

Often the "friends" or family of those so embattled are encouraged to "pull themselves up by their bootstraps," that is, take charge of their life and "quit feeling sorry for yourself." *Depending upon how severely wounded the warrior is by the weapon of despair, it may not be possible to recover without some additional help.* Realistically, a warrior can be so wounded and in despair that his healing will depend in a very large degree upon the faithfulness of God's people to reach out in love, not judgment or condemnation. Many excellent books have been written which can help the struggling warrior, yet the greatest help will come from the investment of time and energy with one or more who are committed to that warrior and his spiritual health. There is a spiritual gift of encouragement and in Galatians 6:2 we are told to carry each others' burdens. The warrior fighting despair needs others to assist him with his burdens.

Christian counselors should also be considered in overcoming despair. Despair and depression are serious and should be taken seriously. Depression can lead to suicide and often becomes chronic without, professional intervention. Your pastor may be able to provide counsel or recommend a qualified counselor. There is no shame in seeing a pastor or

Christian counselor when combating Satan's weapon of despair, or for that matter, when dealing with any serious issue that requires wise input.

As a conclusion to this chapter I want to state clearly that these weapons of Satan's are deadly and claim many victims. However, even as I say that, I also must say that each one of his fiery darts is blocked when the armor of God is fully worn and the weapons of God practiced. Do not lose sight of who truly is in control, for though Satan's power is real, it is only temporary. Isaiah 54:17 assures us that these weapons have no real power except such as we give them.

> "No weapon formed against you will prevail, and you will refute every tongue that accuses you. This is the heritage of the servants of the Lord, and this is their vindication from me, declares the Lord."

Satan's tricks and deceits all come to naught when brought into the light. Be on guard, warrior, for these weapons of the enemy and practice your ability to recognize them for what they are, and respond appropriately.

Questions:

1. Why is despair harder to accept than a disease?

2. How does chronic despair differ from despair caused by crisis?

3. Most, when dealing with despair, resort to blaming themselves or others for their situation. Describe ways to break this cycle and find victory.

4. Discuss the different forms of despair and their effects upon the spiritual warrior.

5. Satan's two goals are stated in the early part of this chapter. What were those goals and why these two goals?

6. Of the four strategies which Satan uses, which is most effective against you and why?

CHAPTER 8
TEARING DOWN DEMONIC STRONGHOLDS

THE MISSHAPEN HEART

Ideally, the heart would become perfect once we are saved and filled with the Holy Spirit. In actuality, although now the heart is free from the guilt of sin and the inner nature which draws one to sin, there still exists the effects of the years when we did not own Christ as Savior, and the imperfection of human flesh. Before we can enter effectively into warfare in the heavenly realms, the sanctified warrior must dwell on the battlefield of the heart long enough to address the warps and bulges of the misshapen heart. Ideally, the heart is perfectly shaped (i.e. free from personality flaws and problems), in reality it has actually been misshapen by a variety of experiences accumulated in the time before Christ became Savior and even afterwards by demonic activity that we did not, and perhaps still do not, recognize as such. Note the illustration on the next page.

Thus, there quite often exists in the sanctified believer, strongholds of demonic influence, which, unless eradicated, will seek to overwhelm us at unexpected moments. The believer is *not* demon possessed, but while these strongholds exist is more receptive to demonic influence. The Israelites, when they were commanded to go into the promised land and completely eliminate all those who inhabited the land. Unfortunately they left some of the people. These are like strongholds not yet conquered in our lives. God's response to the Israelites was:

> "Yet you have disobeyed me. Why have you done this? Now therefore I tell you that I will not drive them out before you; they will be thorns, in your sides and their gods will be a snare to you." Judges 2:2,3

Ideal - A heart pure from committed sin, inbred sin, and demonic strongholds (areas of by demonic strongholds).	Reality - a heart black with committed sin, inbred sin, and warped strongholds in place.	Saved- cleansed from committed sin, but inbred sin is still present and strongholds are in place	Sanctified – committed sins forgiven, inbred sin cleansed, but still warped areas which must be torn down to reach ideal and misshapen places submitted fully to the Lordship of Jesus and the process of holiness

The believer, although saved and sanctified who still has "warped" areas of the heart (strongholds) which now must be brought under the Holy Spirit's control by tearing down the walls and rebuilding them according to the directions of the Spirit. Demonic strongholds deny good growth of the fruit of the spirit, and sap our strength to face the battle as victorious warriors.

Demonic strongholds range from those that are barely surviving to those so firmly in place they are often accepted as a part of our personality. 2 Corinthians 10:3-5 assures us that regardless how deeply entrenched the stronghold is, it can be totally demolished by the power of our weapons:

> "For though we live in the world, we do not wage war as the world does. The weapons we fight with are not the weapons of the world. On the contrary, they have divine power to demolish strongholds. We demolish arguments and every pretension that sets itself up against the knowledge of God and we take captive every thought to make it obedient to Christ."

Again, I am not suggesting that the warrior is demon *possessed*. However, I am stating that many warriors, even sanctified ones, may be demon *influenced*, albeit without their direct knowledge, because they perceive their actions and attitudes as natural due to their background and experiences. It is crucial to realize who controlled the warrior prior to his commitment to Christ, and, thus, from where many of the attitudes and coping mechanisms have evolved. Explicitly, before we came to know Christ as Lord, Satan had time to implant strongholds in the form of habits, ways of thinking and attitudes, not to mention the scars of negative life experiences whose impact is often not felt until years afterwards. This is one reason why it is important to teach our children about Christ and lead them to a saving relationship as early as possible. I was raised in, and served as Pastor of, churches where holiness was a fundamental doctrine and sanctification was preached consistently. Yet it is remarkable that many, if not most of those who claim the experience of full heart holiness, although more loving and committed for the most part, continue to respond to circumstances as they have always done, even when those responses are obviously out of line with scriptural principles. Some recognize the discrepancy between their actions and agonize over the difference, doubting their baptism by the Holy Spirit, even though the work of sanctification was apparent to all. Others see no problem in harmonizing faulty coping mechanisms and attitudes with the presence of the Holy Spirit.

This problem is not restricted to one church but to every one where people are present. Every pastor I talk with shares the same observations; there are few who really understand and live a holy life, yet there are many who have obviously been filled with the Holy Spirit, yet still respond contrary to that filling. While such responses might be and some certainly are due to spiritual immaturity, I believe more have to do with demonic strongholds (i.e. areas of influence) which continue to affect their behavior. Can it be that sanctification is so difficult that only a very few may ever hope to attain the full measure of the experience and the rest must labor and strive towards it without ever achieving this blessing? No, the filling of the Holy Spirit comes by faith, as was stated in another chapter, and a complete abandonment to the will of God in my life. The problem, has nothing to do with commitment, nor God's ability to fill with the Holy Spirit, but with *the shape the heart* has been twisted in the years before salvation. The scars of the past, although covered by the blood, and filled with the Spirit, are still scars which must be dealt with for the warrior to achieve inner victory. These demonic strongholds can take many forms and are peculiar to each individual. Some of the many examples include:

Unbelief	Anxiety
Cold Love	Fear
Un-forgiveness	Lust
Rage	Chemical Dependency
Poor Self-Image	Depression
Bitterness	Apathy
Guilt	Perfectionism
Busyness	Procrastination
Laziness	Jealousy
Disobedience	Gossip
Meanness	Failure
Gluttony	Greed
Selfishness	Pride

Although this is not an entire list, one can easily see that the negatives of our human nature can easily be amplified by demonic forces

Lust

Unforgivenes

Hatred

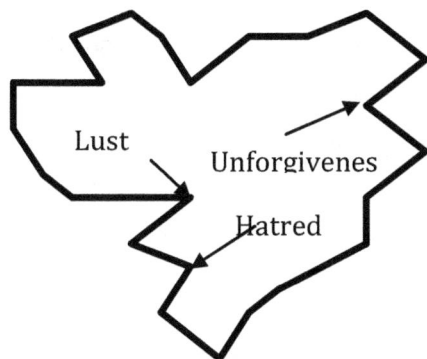

until they become a part of what we consider to be our nature. Note the illustration.

Some will say sanctification takes care of all of these influences immediately, and in some that maybe true, however, for many, the influences or strongholds are not even recognized as areas needing attention let alone cleansing. In tearing down these or any other demonic strongholds we will use a set strategy outlined in detail in the next section.

The tearing down of demonic strongholds should only come as God reveals those strongholds and directs us to their destruction. Thus, the newly sanctified should strive to open himself as much as possible to the illumination of the Holy Spirit by the reading of the word, attendance at public worship and Christian fellowship. When the time is right, if a demonic stronghold exists, God will direct the warrior's efforts to demolish that stronghold. When that happens, the strategy outlined in the next section will assist the warrior in achieving total victory over the stronghold.

Before discussing the strategy for tearing down strongholds, there are a few considerations which have to be addressed:

First: The revelation of a stronghold which needs tearing down will almost invariably come at a time when you feel ill equipped to deal with it. By that I mean God will often reveal a stronghold to you which is affecting your life in the midst of other trauma, physical, emotional or relational in your personal life. The reason for this is that His strength is made perfect in our weakness. We might be tempted to handle the stronghold in our own strength. By coming at a time of personal trauma there is, of course, the temptation to just give up, but for the one who will use spiritual weapons and a spiritual strategy, there is assured victory. Satan will wage war, but the victory is guaranteed to be ours. When we use spiritual weapons and a spiritual strategy, Satan is effectively blocked and the stronghold cannot stand. It will fall.

There will also be the temptation to ignore the prompting of the Holy Spirit and insist that you're fine and that is just "who you are." When "who you are" however, operates outside of the boundaries of love and righteousness then there is likely a stronghold issue.

Second: Although the strategy is fully explained in the next section, once a stronghold is identified, there is a normal desire to eliminate that stronghold immediately. While this is a noble sentiment, often the stronghold has been in place for years and our new strength and capability with spiritual weapons is not able to overcome immediately, thus, the need for a careful strategy. This delay between identification of a stronghold and the actual tearing down of the stronghold can be frustrating for the Christian and is often used by Satan as a secondary front of attack. The Christian must realize at the onset that God not only understands the delay but will continue to assist in the defeat of the stronghold. He is a God of mercy and compassion.

Third: This strategy calls for certain steps to be followed. Depending on the individual and the stronghold's grip on the individual, each step will be moved through at different rates of speed. Speed itself is not the goal. There is no asset to racing through the steps only to have to redo them. Better to accomplish each goal fully before moving on to the next.

Finally, before moving into the actual strategy, I want to re-emphasize the weapons of our warfare:

Praise--Praising God with spoken word, with a life lived in love, but especially in singing before the Lord.

Prayer--conversation with God builds the relationship and provides guidance and strength.

Perseverance --Someone once said, "If you think you can't, you're right, but if you think you can, you're also right." Satan's goal is to persuade you to quit.

Perspective --Continue to have the mind of Christ and the knowledge that we do not war against flesh and blood, but against the principalities and powers of this dark age.

Performance --What we *do* shouts louder than what we *say*. Show your love for Christ by loving others as He did. No warrior will ever be fulfilled until he finds and begins to use his spiritual gifts in service to others.

Questions:

1. When an individual quits smoking, the effects of that behavior do not immediately leave the body. Just so, when saved, the impact of our old lifestyle will still be found in demonic strongholds. Bringing the heart back to an ideal shape is an ongoing process. Describe some of the ways your old lifestyle has impacted your heart and the possible strongholds you face.

STRATEGY FOR TEARING DOWN DEMONIC STRONGHO1DS

The strategy outlined in this section has proven effective in demolishing demonic strongholds that stand in opposition to God's design for our lives. You should move through this strategy at God's direction but remember at every step to have your weapons at hand and your armor in place.

1.   Realize and admit that we are powerless in our own strength to overcome demonic strongholds.

"I'll get right with God after I get my life straightened out," goes a popular quote. The "I can do it myself" philosophy fostered by our society has kept many powerless who could be powerful warriors. Realistically, there are some things which require assistance, tearing down demonic strongholds is one of those. Perhaps a good insight here comes from David when he cries out "Lead me to the rock that is higher than I." (Psalm 61:2) He was beset by demons who were stronger, more cunning and more wily than himself. So, too, are we. To even attempt to overcome these demonic strongholds in our own strength allows the demon of pride access to our hearts and, if left unchecked, will result in defeat and discouragement. As God reveals demonic strongholds in our lives we are confronted with a choice. The obvious choice is to go forward and begin the destruction of the stronghold; yet we must realize that some of those strongholds have been in place for decades and the foundation is deep and its impact on the personality seems too complex to eliminate. Many shy away from considering what has been revealed as a demonic stronghold saying, "That's just the way I am."

Denial is one of the strongest defenses of any demonic stronghold, and one we cling to as a personal defense of our ego. When first confronted with a problem, our response is to deny the problem, or our role in it if possible, and supply excuses for the problem if not. Thus, individuals have struggled for years battling demons that could be destroyed if only they were acknowledged. My sons were visiting my parents one summer when they were very young. My mother took them to the park for an afternoon of fun. The day was overcast and she didn't think too much about them being out for so long...until that evening when huge blisters began to rise on one of her grandson's ears. The ultraviolet rays pierced the overcast sky to provide a memorable sunburn. Demonic strongholds have much the same impact. It does not *seem* as if there is much of a problem, at least as far as we are concerned, so why worry about it? The reality is that much harm can be, and is being, done, especially as a negative influence for others who need Christ. Additionally, many have been persuaded to turn away from their faith by the influence, subtly and insistently presented the strongholds in their life. To deny their existence is to move to the head of the list as a candidate for failure.

The solution begins when we recognize there actually is a problem. Yet, even after accomplishing this monumental step, we must be wary of a sneak attack from the demon of pride who will try to convince us to handle our problem on our own. "You don't need to bother God with this, it's not that big a deal, you can lick it by yourself if you really try," the demon suggests. Unfortunately, this lie consigns many, who might otherwise

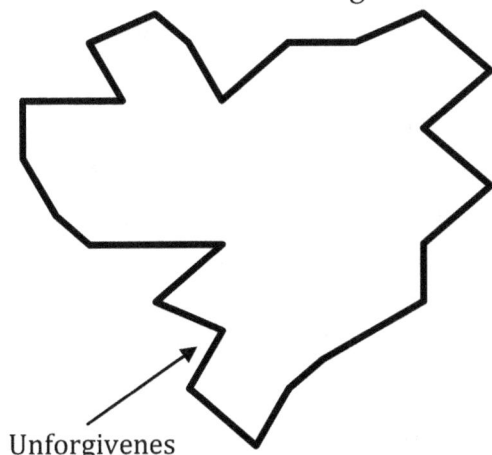

Unforgivenes

be powerful warriors, to constant struggling and frustrations in their personal lives.

The Holy Spirit will reveal strongholds which needs to be demolished. Remember Psalm 61: 2b where David prays to be led to a rock that is higher than he is? That is where we too must go. If indeed you are dealing with a demonic stronghold you will not be successful in destroying it in your own power. Let me repeat that; you will not be successful in defeating a demonic stronghold in your own power. Romans 7:18-24 sets forth the struggle which affects even the staunchest Christian who tries to be victorious on his own strength.

> "I know that nothing good lives in me, that is, in my sinful nature. For I have the desire to do what is good, but I cannot carry it out. For what I do is not the good I want to do; no, the evil I do not want to do--this I keep on doing. Now if I do what I do not want to do, it is no longer I who do it, but it is sin living in me that does it. So I find this law at work: When I want to do good, evil is right there with me. For in my inner being I delight in God's law; but I see another law at work in the members of my body, waging war against the law of my mind and making me a prisoner of the law of sin at work within my members. What a wretched man I am! Who will rescue me from this body of death?"

Yet, to admit that we actually are flawed and powerless could lead to despair were it not for the following steps. By the same token, the following strategy is meaningless unless we come fully to grips with our impotence to handle the stronghold revealed. I suggest you pause here and begin a soul searching process, asking the Holy Spirit to reveal such strongholds in your personal life as God would have you deal with now.

Note: you are NOT required to have demonic strongholds in your life. Not everyone has demonic strongholds, and many who did have them were set free from their influence at the time of their baptism in the Holy Spirit. It is not necessary to manufacture strongholds that then must be broken down. Wait on the Holy Spirit and be open to His leading. If, any strongholds exist, they will be revealed to you as you are able in God's estimation to deal with them.

2. *Believe that God can destroy the stronghold.*

Here it is not enough to just recite a mental litany of belief, or even a verbal assent to God's abilities. Our society has encouraged an attitude which is willing to say whatever they think we want to hear, while blithely going their own way. To follow this step requires a little more from us than a simple "I believe." For the warrior to be truly effective against the demon he is confronting, he must move to the belief that affects the very nature of his reality. No more, "That's just the way I am, like it or lump it." Now the warrior asserts that "I have a problem but I believe that God can totally heal me from these demonic attacks and influence." Belief of this nature yields to God the sovereignty of my will and makes Him ruler in more than name. A God who is powerful enough to defeat my demons deserves my allegiance. He is my King and my Lord.

We have come this far in the battle having made the decision to believe. We believed on Christ for salvation. We believed again and received the Holy Spirit. Woe to the warrior who then feels he has arrived. The battle demands constant faith in the commander, Jesus Christ. It is He who will lead you in the destruction of this demonic stronghold. It is He who empowers your weapons with supernatural energy. It is in His name that the stronghold will be defeated. However, if we allow the demon of doubt to have access, we may be persuaded that it's just too hard. We have targeted the stronghold, be it fear, or rage, hurtful habits, etc. We know where it is God wants us to advance, but... An illustration of how doubt can delay deliverance may be seen in Israel's history during the Exodus when the tribe of Israel, after being delivered from the Egyptians approached the new land that God had promised them. Moses, the commander, sent out twelve men to spy out the land. They returned with stories of a wonderful land, peopled by warriors. Ten of the men recommended that they not attempt to go in, for the way looked too hard. Two men said "We can do this." The people listened to the ten .and God sent them back into the desert for forty years until everyone of that generation who refused to believe that God could deliver them had died (c.f. Deuteronomy 1,2)

True belief is no small thing. Yet true belief will move the warrior into a strategic position for striking down the enemy.

3.   *Make the decision to turn that stronghold over to God.*

The first two steps of the strategy deal with a mental assent to the process, now we move into the area of the will. Making the decision to turn the stronghold over to God goes beyond the acknowledgment that we have a problem, or even that God can handle the problem. As difficult as it was to acknowledge that there is a demonic stronghold controlling part of your life, many still struggle with making that decision to turn it over to God.

Here is where your faith is tested and here is where Satan's attacks begin to mount. It is that demon's home that you are threatening. Be it fear, pride, a past experience, or some destructive habit, he will use whatever means at his disposal to discourage you from tearing down his secure hold on your life. His argument may run, "That's just the way you are, don't get so religious," or "You really want to change but let's wait to start changing until...." A favorite ploy of demons is to re-direct you to a seemingly more immediate problem. These usually take the form of a health problem, a marital problem, financial difficulties, job problems, etc. If you succumb to his diversion, then you will actually be moved back to step one in the strategy. Crucial here is the weapon of "perspective." The warrior must be assured in his heart that the battle is not against flesh and blood--no matter the pain, no matter the anguish. If a demon can get you side-tracked onto another problem area, or delayed, he will do so to preserve his own influence.

Because those diversions will seek to turn your attention elsewhere, it will take energy for the warrior to stay focused. Each step of the strategy becomes the crucial step when you arrive at that point. Too many times we are diverted from our real objectives into situations that bog us down. Wielding the weapon of perspective, realize that your war is not these diversions, but a very real struggle with a demonic stronghold. Come to that place of inner resolve which will stand as a testimony of your intent for the demon to read clearly his impending doom. As the Patriarchs raised their altars at decision points in their lives in honor to the God they chose to follow, so make the decision to stand on an altar representing your decision to go God's way no matter what. Maintain your perspective and persevere in your decision to turn this stronghold over God. BUT DON'T STOP HERE. At each step, the temptation will be to believe what you have done is sufficient to accomplish victory . . . but its not. Cementing the victory requires even more.

4. *Make a soul-searching list of how this stronghold is in control of my life.*

Now that you have definitely decided to turn the stronghold over to God, it's time to look within yourself and take inventory of what this stronghold has done to you and those you love. This will not be an easy step and you might be inclined to skip over this part, or to spend too little time here. To do so is to underestimate your enemy, a dangerous practice for anyone who doesn't want to be caught from behind. However, introspection of one's failings in any area has the possibility of leaving the individual discouraged and despairing of victory, thus, before you begin, take the following precautions:

1. Spend some time praising God (listening and singing along with praise music is helpful).

2. Read a section of God's word (until you sense His peace).

3. Pray. Here you ask God to reveal the damage, but here you also testify to the Lord that you have made a decision that:

    a. you believe He is able to totally demolish the stronghold,

    b. you need His support and strength to succeed.

    c. you turn this stronghold over to Him for destruction.

Now you are ready! While some will attempt this process in their head, the real value of this step comes when you can get alone at the kitchen table or wherever and actually put down on paper what you discern and what God reveals to you. As the list grows you will begin to understand the true nature of the demon that is encamping around your heart. You will see the effects of his attacks for what they have done to you and to your loved ones. Caution should be taken here for now the demon will try to throw all the blame on you with accusations such as, "See how awful you really are?" "How could God love someone like you?" "See what harm you have done to God's temple, your body?" "You don't deserve His love, why don't you just realize it and quit?" On and on go his lies. Taking authority in Jesus' name, rebuke that demon, following the practice outlined in Chapter 6. Remember, you are threatening his existence. Do not allow his accusations to turn this list into a *document of self blame*, but, use the list as *indictment* for demonic destruction. Place it before God in prayer on the altar of your decision.

Some of the ways it can affect me:

- I harbor anger towards another.

- I feel sorry for myself.

- I have a broken relationship.

- I am patterning un-forgiveness to my family and friends.

- I am affecting how others think about the one I haven't forgiven.

- I dwell on the wrong done to keep the un-forgiveness alive.

- My soul is not at peace and I have a hard time contacting God.

5. Confess to God, myself, and to another human the exact nature of the stronghold's influence on my life.

As John Wesley discovered in his small group meetings, the act of confession is not only scriptural (James 5:16 reads, "Therefore confess your sins to each other and pray for each other so that you may be healed. The prayer of a righteous man is powerful and effective."), but provides many assets to the warrior.

a. There is a sense of accountability when one confesses a stronghold to someone else. After confession, there is an inner awareness that someone knows, and will hold you accountable. Accountability is another word that is frequently used, but avoided in actual practice whenever possible. Accountability is not only desirable, for it produces actual results, but also practical in that the warrior is not concealing or hiding sin.

b. Confession to another allows their participation in prayerful support. When confession is made to another Christian, their prayers in your behalf often prove decisive in the final victory. Their support and encouragement will often be timely enough to help you resist demonic attacks. Scripture indicates that there is power when two are agreed on any point.

> Matthew 18:19,20, "Again, I tell you that if two of you on earth agree about anything you ask for, it will be done for you by my father in heaven. For where two or three come together in my name, there am I with them."

This fact comes into play mightily when you join together with another not only in confession, but in prayer for demonic stronghold destruction.

c. In the act of confession the exact nature of the stronghold and it's influence is placed in the proper perspective. The demon of that stronghold will have made his stronghold either appear too formidable to tear down or too insignificant to bother with. By opening your life to another you may receive a new picture of that stronghold which often is nearer to reality. There is no stronghold too secure or formidable for God to tear down, nor is there any insignificant stronghold, especially since you were directed to it's destruction by the Holy Spirit.

d. By confessing in this manner you are following the commands of God's word and, thus, humbling yourself to the authority of God (James 5:16). This is no mean feat. Many come to this point and are unwilling to proceed because they refuse this confession. Many reasons are usually given but the bottom line in such refusal is pride. If God's word says to do so, and it does, then there is no valid excuse for refusal. Any such refusal becomes rebellion against God, no matter the excuse. For too long we Christians have rationalized the untrustworthiness of others, a lack of time, or simple weariness for our unwillingness to submit ourselves fully to God's word, particularly at this point.

Admittedly there are certain standards that should be observed by the one hearing the confession.

A. Anything confessed should be held in strict confidence. That means no talking! Not as a prayer request, not as the "truth," not at all! The only exception is when immediate, physical, harm might result to the individual confessing or to someone else if such information is not forwarded to a responsible person. Even in a case where immediate harm might result, the one hearing the confession should restrict the information only to absolutely essential personnel.

B. The one hearing the confession must refrain from preaching, judging, or acting shocked. What the one confessing needs is compassion, support, and prayer. Advice, if offered at all, should be secondary. Too often we begin to preach, citing scripture to support our judgment and guidance. What a wonderful thing to have a friend who will simply accept you as you are, without preaching, and love you anyway.

C. Prayer. If you have heard someone's confession of a struggle with a stronghold, it should become a part of your daily prayer life. Remembering that individual daily in prayer will greatly assist their struggle toward victory, for it marshals the forces in a realm which cannot be seen but is far more real than the existence we presently have.

D. Be genuinely concerned. To never ask the individual how they are doing or express support is a direct denial of God's word that we should love each other better than ourselves. Worse, it indicates in a language much louder than words they are not important to us.

Do not hesitate to periodically check on how the warrior is doing and encourage him in his battle.

The use of a confessor does not negate Christ's role as our high priest, nor does it lessen our own ability or responsibility to come before God ourselves in prayer. God placed Adam with Eve because He saw that we need each other. It's OK for you to lean on someone else in the midst of your conflict. In leaning on a friend you will become strong enough for someone else to lean upon you in their battle.

6. *Let go of all that the stronghold means.*

A story is told that monkeys are caught by tying a hollowed-out coconut shell with a small hole in it just barely large enough for a monkey's flattened hand to enter to a tree with something inside that can only come out if dislodged and brought out. The monkey, intrigued by this odd coconut and a desirable bauble, sticks his hand in the small hole and clasps the trinket, only to find he cannot remove his hand because the hole is now too small for his clenched fist to pass through. The monkey will refuse to let the item go, even though he could be freed by simply opening his hand, and so is caught. So, we also face this great challenge, "I know I can't let go myself, Lord," we say, "I know You can help me let go, I have decided to let go, I've made a list and know I must let go. I've even confessed to someone else that I want to let go, but..." Now is where the rubber of our decision meets the road of reality. If your resolve was firm and sincere and each of the steps was completed in the same way, then step six, although difficult, will not be impossible, precisely because you have brought Jesus into the situation. Let go of your right to maintain the thought and/or hurt for even one entire second. To entertain the thought and/or pain for one second opens the door for two seconds, and then three, and then four

"But there surely is no harm in just thinking about 'it,'" you say. Not so, for as a man thinks so is he. Satan must flee when we resist. When we entertain him he takes over like the cat in the children's story of The Cat in the Hat. Unclench you fist, finger by finger if necessary, but let go of that stronghold. Some will be tempted here to draw this out; to make the letting go a gradual experience. There is, however, a real danger in following a delaying tactic. First of all, you should have already been cutting back on the stronghold's influence from the first moment it was revealed to you. To continue the gradual withdrawal now is an attempt at deceiving yourself, or allowing yourself to be deceived by the stronghold's influence. Now, right now, by the power of the name of Jesus, let go completely.

Following through with letting go often leaves the warrior with a strong sense of vulnerability. It is a good idea to remember here the defensive stance described in Chapter Five and to have that armor in place. Again, I would strongly urge you not to linger here but to press immediately on to step seven.

7.   *Ask God to destroy the stronghold and its foundations.*

I like to watch the demolition of large buildings on television. It's amazing to me how they can set the charges to bring down those multi-storied buildings so that the rubble is piled all together instead of blown all apart. Yet, after the explosion, comes the mundane work of hauling away the rubble. Once you get to the bottom of the pile, though there is still a foundation that is planted deep into the ground, deep enough to provide a secure base for the once impressive building. In the same fashion the demonic strongholds in our lives are built on foundations that up to this point have provided a secure base. *If the stronghold is destroyed but the foundation is left, the job has not been completed.*

Eradication of foundations requires my willingness and active participation to purge from my lifestyle every vestige of influence from that stronghold. Total removal means a change in lifestyle, often as significant as the change which occurs at salvation. It may mean:

- Changing the television programming watched

- Taking a clear stand with your friends and possibly even changing the company kept or the job held.

- Walking or driving down a different street to avoid being exposed to certain temptations

- Eliminating or blocking certain internet sites.

- etc.

Do you desperately and absolutely crave deliverance from this stronghold? If so, ask God to destroy its influence in your life, to completely dismantle it--including the foundation on which it stands. For some this will mean a radically new lifestyle, for others a break with old friends and practices. In each case it means a sense of freedom.

This step is the full release of the power of the Holy Spirit. The Holy Spirit has always had the power to do this for you. Now, after following the strategy outlined above, you are finally ready. The power of the Holy Spirit demolishes the demonic stronghold down to it's foundations. However, the warrior must be aware that while he is no longer controlled by that stronghold, there will be temptation to submit again to that influence. Remember, temptation is a part of every warrior's existence. Again, I refer you to Chapter Five which deals with the armor of God.

The stronghold is demolished but there may be the possibility that this area might be an Achilles heal which will need to be guarded against in the future. Take heart, we're almost through the strategy which will clean up all the rubble that remains. What? Clean up rubble? Yuck! That's right, there are some remains that must be disposed of and a new structure built on the old site. The next few steps will walk you through this process.

8.   *Make a list of all those who were harmed by the expression of the stronghold and/or those whose words or actions started the stronghold and be willing to make amends or forgive.*

Note: at this point we are discussing developing a willingness to make amends or forgive, and a specific target audience. As you continue in your prayer life, the Holy Spirit will reveal to you certain individuals who have suffered in some way because of the stronghold's influence in your life. The Holy Spirit will also reveal individuals whose verbal or physical abuse created an opening for the stronghold to be constructed. This list may be lengthy or short, but every name the Holy Spirit brings to mind is important! The list may include individuals who have died. Whoever the Holy Spirit brings to mind, dead or alive, write down that name. It is important to trust His guidance at this point.

We could liken what is happening now to a surgical procedure for the removal of a bullet. In step seven the bullet was removed The wound must be cleansed, and body stitched back together. This step begins the healing of the soul. It begins the process of rubble removal that will allow the warrior to go on with his life.

Now that you have your list, given by the Holy Spirit's guidance, go over each name and search your heart for any reservation in making amends or forgiving. Be much in prayer over each incident God brings to mind. It is not possible to eliminate names; remember they came from a higher source. Take those names marked with reservation before the Lord in prayer. God will help you understand the source of your reservation and teach you an important lesson in humility and forgiveness. If you have been reading the word, God will assist you.

After working through the willingness issue, you may be tempted to believe you are finished. This temptation must be resisted! Move on to step nine and the actual making of amends/forgiveness.

9. *Make restitution wherever possible.*

After completing step eight, step nine will go much smoother than you might imagine. There are some things to watch out for:

A. Be on your guard against procrastination.

B. In making amends, be honest and transparent about what you have done and why you are now coming forward to make amends.

C. Do not be defensive or offer excuses for your behavior. Defensiveness is merely another form of denial. It is imperative that the warrior steer away from any form of denial if healing is to occur.

D. Remember to respond in love, regardless of how you are responded to in return.

E. In forgiving, be honest about the feelings which resulted from the verbal or physical abuse. If you are afraid that harm might come to you if you were to express these feelings, write the words out, even if the offending party never sees them. Being open and honest paves the way for true forgiveness. David Seamands book, *Healing for Damaged Emotions* is particularly helpful in dealing with scars of the past.

For many, the thought of making amends will mean a queasy stomach and thoughts of confrontation. No one likes confrontation, or at least most try to avoid it, still, making amends need not be confrontational.

As you work through your list, you will sense a great burden being lifted off your shoulders. The conscience is well aware in it's bookkeeping to whom you owe something and who owes you, even if it's only a thank you or a simple apology. Making amends or forgiving balances an internal scale. A stronghold demolished brings the believer closer into contact with God and broadens his usefulness in the battle

For those on your list who have died, I have a tried and true suggestion. Sit down and write that person a letter, expressing all your feelings. Say the things you wish you could say to them in person were they still alive. Place it in an envelope and then give it to the one you have used as a friend and confessor to dispose of as they see fit.

10. Build an altar of worship and praise on the ground where that stronghold stood.

This is an exciting opportunity! As you begin to build an altar to God, start with praise, glorifying the One who has set you free. Take plenty of time here. Praise is one of your weapons and now is the time to show how well you have learned its use. Praise God for your deliverance and rejoice in His mighty work. Like a parade is a big event, make your praises a "big event". As you move from praise, lay an altar of consecration down.

This was a pattern throughout Jewish history after a remarkable event and one we would do better to follow more often. Set a stone of remembrance so that when you see it you will be reminded of what God has done for you. The "stone of remembrance" will have a double purpose. First, it will remind you that the demon's power over you is broken, regardless of the demon's attempts to persuade you otherwise. Second, it will strengthen your resolve to go forward with God.

Continue in prayer, consecrating yourself as a holy vessel for the use of the Lord. Pray expecting God will renew your filling of the Holy Spirit. One of the exciting lessons from the New Testament is that the Holy Spirit came and filled those who prayed in total consecration on more than one occasion. There is no doubt in my mind, as a good friend of mine reminds me, "Christians leak." Warriors need an occasional "re-filling," especially when dealing a final blow to a demonic stronghold.

11. Share your testimony of victory with others who need to hear it.

The truth in Romans 8:28 is borne out over and over again. The pain of our lives has provided untold thousands the resources to reach out and help others with similar pain. As a warrior for the cross, your challenge will be to open yourself to the Holy Spirit's use so that when God leads you to someone who has gone through what you have, you will be able to assist them.

Our ability to serve God through use of our experiences provides meaning in an otherwise meaningless struggle. Yet, there is some risk, for in helping someone else, you open yourself up to be hurt, rejected, or used. Truly, the warrior who recognizes the threat and perseveres in his ministry is the one who has learned what it means to be an instrument of God's love.

ONE FINAL NOTE

Before I conclude this chapter I must remind you of the difference between demonic strongholds and the temptations which have been discussed earlier. There *is* a difference. The demonic stronghold has exerted subtle influences which *have* warped *and are* warping your life which typically are holdovers from your life in the prison mode, i.e. before salvation. Temptations are influences which attempt to affect your life. They may be subtle or as blatant as a brass band. Just because you have defeated the demonic stronghold in Jesus' Name does not mean you will never be tempted in that area again. In fact, you may be repeatedly tempted until you show that your armor is tight against that temptation. David Seamands provides an excellent illustration of the necessity for tearing down these strongholds drawn from Os Guinness' book In Two Minds:

> "Picture healthy faith as a person who has a firm grip so he can reach out and take hold of anything he wants to. Now imagine that this person has an open wound in the palm of his hand. The object he desires to hold is in front of him, and his muscular strength is sufficient. But the unbearable pain which will result makes it very difficult or even impossible to grasp the object. This is exactly what happens to many Christians with unhealed emotional scars. The very process of trying to believe exerts great pressure on an emotional wound that is too painful to bear. In fact, the questions of doubts which seem to be coming from their *heads* are actually arising out of some deeply buried hurts in their *hearts.*"[37]

One preacher I listened to kept repeating, "different levels, different devils." It is clear to me that this reference applies to the warrior growing strong in the Lord. As he successfully overcomes demonic attacks and strongholds the enemy mounts ever more insidious attacks. What the

---

[37]David A. Seamands, Healing of Memories (Victor Books, 1985), 114

enemy refuses to accept is that he has already lost. The true warrior is well equipped to handle such attacks and perseveres in the battleground of the heart knowing one day he will stand before the throne of God. Because he is well prepared and strong in battle, the warrior is also able to wage war on a second front: Warfare in the Heavenlies.

Questions

1. Define demonic strongholds

2. Explain how a demonic stronghold might exist in the life of a sanctified warrior.

3. How can Satan use denial to defeat the warrior?

4. Have you discovered a demonic stronghold in your life? and have you begun it's destruction?

5. Why is confession avoided by many warriors? What would make confession easier?

6. What is the role of the Holy Spirit in stronghold destruction?

CHAPTER 9
WAR IN THEHEAVENLIES

I have attempted in the preceding chapters to provide the warrior with a base from which to achieve victory in spiritual warfare on the battleground of the heart. I wish someone had shared these principles, weapons, and strategies with me at an earlier age. The warrior who truly grasps all that is contained in this work and uses these concepts consistently will find that he is ready and even eager for greater challenges. I would like to touch upon some of those challenges in the final pages of this book. No attempt is made here to deal with these challenges thoroughly. Others have written about their understanding of this phase of spiritual warfare. The Holy Spirit is still teaching me in these areas and when the time is right, another book will be written about the battle in the heavenlies. Not only will this not be a thorough look at war in the heavenlies, but I do not claim to even mention each part of that war, nor to be an authority on any part. I can only mention what I know or what has been revealed to me.

Also, much of the warfare in heavenly realms is accomplished through the exercise of spiritual gifts, about which I have only lightly touched upon in this work. One who has accepted Christ some time ago may be familiar with spiritual gifts even to the point of considering them to be mundane. That would be a mistake. Spiritual gifts are given to bring out an individual's fullest potential for the accomplishment of the mission. While we all serve a broad mission given by Jesus, each local ministry further defines that mission for their specific situations and locale. The fulfillment of the mission is the ultimate work of the warrior and the context for his warfare in heavenly realms. Spiritual gifts, rightly understood and applied, make such war fare possible. Some of the more prominent parts of that battleground are mentioned below.

INTERCESSION

Intercession, though not normally viewed as warfare in the heavenlies, will be a major part or the warrior's prayer life from the moment he enters the battle. In spite of that, I include it here because there is an aspect of intercession which requires a fully equipped warrior who has been gifted by God for this ministry. Intercession at this level, as all of the other aspects, requires a willingness to sacrifice personal pleasure and comfort in order to achieve the goal.

Intercession is an aspect of prayer that causes the warrior to stand in the "gap" so that God may make a connection with the person or subject of intercession. The intercessor may become the physical "conductor" of God's touch, the spiritual "conductor," or both. As an electric current passes through some materials while having no effect upon others, not every warrior will become accomplished at this important part of the battle. Some conductors pass electricity, but are of a size or shape which makes the connection erratic or with greater or lesser voltage. For the warrior who has the gift of intercession, the ability to carry the burden of keeping the connection intact comes naturally. Still, the gift of intercessional prayer requires discipline and further training to bring out the fullest results. It also demands a heavy toll from the warrior. The intercessor will feel the burden of the one he intercedes for as well as the proximity of a Holy God. The connection for which the intercessor pleads is dictated by the Holy Spirit. For some it will be for the salvation of a soul, for another, safety in a specific situation, etc. The one who practices this gift will accomplish powerful results, yet may never see the fruit of his labors. Many missionaries speak of how God kept them in safety or provided a revival spirit where many were saved. Others tell of how they were at the end of their own resources and ready to end it all when they found themselves near a church, or listening to a Christian broadcast, or reading a Bible. I believe that such testimonies come because somewhere God has a warrior interceding for a specific need.

MIRACLES

Miracles are even harder to describe than intercession, and may even be too broad a topic. The gift of miracles is listed as a spiritual gift in 1 Corinthians 12:10, "to another miraculous powers,..." No explanation is attached, nor is there any clear definition elsewhere. In Acts 4:30 the disciples and new Christians pray, asking God to, "Stretch out your hand to heal and perform miraculous signs and wonders through the name of your holy servant Jesus." Their prayer was part of a petition for greater boldness in proclaiming the gospel. According to the record in Acts, that prayer was answered in powerful ways. Jesus used miracles to draw attention to His message. Many of today's Christians seem content, however, to believe that the day of miracles is past, or relate miracles to an area called "science." I believe God still performs miracles, and that there are warriors who have the gift of miraculous powers. It seems clear to me that the intent of miracles is not the expression of power for powers' sake, but to draw attention to the message. In the ministries of Jesus, Peter, and Paul, miraculous signs were not only tangible expressions of God's love for a hurting people, but were also used as a means of drawing a crowd for the proclamation of the message. Because of the nature of such a gift, the one who exercises it is constantly exposed to Satan's attacks to subvert that gift by suggesting the warrior use the gift outside of God's direction. I have seen miracles happen, I have heard the testimonies of others who have seen miracles. I believe that when we enter into warfare in the heavenlies God will use those warriors He has so gifted to draw attention to the work of the church so that He will be glorified.

HEALING

I am a firm believer in healing. Not just the healing possible from proper medical care, but true miraculous healing where only God gets the glory. Let me quickly add, I believe God uses the medical profession to work out much of the healing of our day. However, I am convinced that there would be more miraculous healings if there were more warriors who would pay the price for this gift. It is my belief from my studies that healing is God's rule, not the exception. That there are exceptions goes without saying, but they are the exceptions, not the rule.

Probably no other part of spiritual warfare is so misunderstood as that which deals with healing. The frailty of life and our bodies' health confronts everyone sooner or later. What part should divine healing play in that confrontation? Isaiah recounts the story of Hezekiah's illness which was to result in death. Hezekiah's prayers, we are told, brought about divine intervention and healing, however, because of that healing there were negative consequences for Israel in the future. Yet others, people we know well to be lovers of Jesus, sicken and die. How does divine healing fit into our battle?

The warrior who exercises this gift will see in scripture how Jesus healed one by a word of faith, another with the touch of a hand, and another with mud made from His saliva. 1 Corinthians 12:9 identifies healing as specific spiritual gift. When Jesus sent out the seventy, recorded in Luke 10, they were admonished to make healing part of their evangelistic work. "When you enter a town and are welcomed, eat what is set before you. Heal the sick who are there and tell them, 'The kingdom of God is near you.'" (Luke 10:8-9). Healing not only is an effective way to draw a crowd, but affects the Readiness Quotient (RQ – discussed earlier) level of an individual. No indication is given in Luke that there are certain, illnesses which the disciples were to avoid in their healing efforts, implying that all illnesses are under God's control. People with all types of illnesses and deformities were brought to Jesus. Never once does scripture record that He was unable to affect a cure. If fact, on one occasion when the disciples were unable to cast out a demon affecting a child's health, Jesus expresses annoyance at the disciples for not being able to handle what, seemingly, should have been a minor difficulty.

> "A man in the crowd called out, "Teacher, I beg you to look at my son, for he is my only child. A spirit seizes him and he suddenly screams; it throws him into convulsions so that he foams at the mouth. It scarcely ever leaves him and is destroying him. I begged your disciples to drive it out, but they could not.' Oh unbelieving and perverse generation, 'Jesus replied, 'how long shall I stay with you and put up with you? Bring your son here. 'Even while the boy was coming the demon threw him to the ground in a convulsion. But Jesus rebuked the evil spirit, healed the boy and gave him back to his father. And they were all amazed at the greatness of God." (Luke 9:3843)

Matthew's version of this healing recalls the disciples inquiring why they were ineffective in the healing of the boy, to which Jesus replies, "Because you have so little faith. I tell you the truth, if you have faith as small as a mustard seed, you can say to this mountain, 'Move from here to there' and it will move. Nothing will be impossible for you." (Matthew 17:20-21) Healing, then, becomes a matter not of impossibility, but of faith. James supports this thesis by writing, "Is any one of you sick? He should call the elders of the church to pray over him and anoint him with oil in the name of the Lord. And the prayer offered in faith will make the sick person well; the Lord will raise him up." (James 5:14-15, emphasis added)

Yet, as was mentioned earlier, many who are individuals of faith are not healed. I believe the difference comes in the battleground of the heavenlies and the warrior who is gifted in healing. Much study and prayer needs to go into this aspect of warfare and it's role today.

EXORCISM

Obviously, if you do not believe in demon possession, you will not consider exorcism part of legitimate warfare, however as it was a part of Jesus' ministry, so too must it be a part of the church's ministry today. When reading stories of the mission field or listening to missionaries speak, one occasionally hears about how a demon was cast out of someone. While this makes for an interesting story, few, if any, of us want to consider the reality of a demonic presence much closer to home. Even television movies and the entire genre of horror films which emphasize the workings of demonic forces, are seen as merely fiction. One of the most frightening aspects of such movies is not the actual images, but that those who wrote the scripts, and to a lesser degree those acting the parts, must have opened themselves to a darker world than most want to believe exist. Demons are real and their influence is felt in every part of the world, even, and perhaps especially, in America. There is little doubt in my mind that most of us know, or know of someone, that when the days are accomplished for judgment, will be revealed as possessed by one or more demons. Similarly, many of those commonly thought to be possessed will be seen to simply be unregenerate or having a demonic stronghold, but not possessed.

The capable warrior will be sensitive to demonic presence and knowledgeable about how to confront and take authority over demons. He will operate in a realm where most fear to tread and many would run from.

OTHER

The other areas of warfare in the heavenlies are no less important than the above mentioned areas. The lists of spiritual gifts found in Romans 12, 1 Corinthians 12, Ephesians 4, etc. set forth many areas of advanced warfare. 1 Corinthians 12:7-11 is the most thorough list.

> "Now to each one the manifestation of the Spirit is given for the common good. To one there is given through the Spirit the *message of wisdom*, to another the *message of knowledge* by means of the same Spirit, to another *faith* by the same Spirit, to another *gifts of healing* by that one Spirit to another *miraculous powers*, to another *prophecy*, to another *distinguishing between spirits*, to another *speaking in different kinds of tongues*, and to still another the *interpretation of tongues*. All these are the work of one and the same Spirit, and he gives them to each one, just as he determines." (bold italics added)

The problem we find as spiritual warriors is not that there are no exciting challenges left in our day, but that there are too few warriors willing to pay the price to enter the battle in heavenly realms. Warfare in heavenly realms always has as it's ultimate goal the fulfillment of the mission. While the battle ground for the heart is a largely personal one, the larger picture brings the warrior into a mosaic where his contributions are noticeable in the kingdom's business.

CHAPTER 10
CONCLUSION

It is, or should be, the goal of each true warrior of the cross to make his Commander proud. Occasionally the church has been burdened with a legalism which hinders the mission and causes attrition among the warriors. Legalism focuses on rules and is really about the exercise of power. The way of Christ lies through the exercise of LOVE and finds its power is sacrifice.

If not legalism, then a liberalism which waters down or ignores the true mission of Christ if often present. liberalism seems to focus on acceptance which is construed to be a focus on love. This is a classic misdirection. The true focus of liberalism is also about power directed at who is and is not accepted (more rules hidden in a language of tolerance).

Thus, I want to say in these final lines that God's requirement of the warrior is to simply do his best--and that your best is usually far beyond your imagination. Often we see our best to be of little importance. *Let God be the judge of what is or is not important.* You are human: you are going to make mistakes and even fail. Even if you were perfect you live around other humans and you can be assured they will NOT be perfect. That is where grace comes in. God's grace is sufficient, even when we are the most human. Accept His grace and your own imperfection even as you continue to work out your salvation with fear and trembling.

Simply walk forward as best you can in the understanding and light He gives you, regardless of where others walk, and you will be a true warrior, worthy of the Commander's sacrifice. Remember, the ultimate commandment is to Love God, and love our neighbor.

BIBLIOGRAPHY

Anderson, Niel, *Victory Over Darkness: Realizing the Power of Your Identity in Christ,* Stewart, Ed, ed., Ventura, CA, Regal Books, 1990

Barna, George, *The Power of Vision,* Ventura, CA, Regal Books, 1992

Bounds, E.M., Power *Through Prayer,* Springdale, PA, Whitaker House,1982

Dods, Marcus, "The Gospel of St. John," W Robertson Nicoll, ed., *TheExpositor's Greek Testament Volume **One**,* Grand Rapids, Wm. B. Erdmans Publishing House, reprinted 1974

Earle, Ralph, *Sanctification in the New Testament* ,Kansas City: Beacon Hill Press, 1988

Frangipane, Francis, *The Three Battlegrounds,* River of Life Ministries, Cedar Rapids, IA, 1989

Greathouse, William M., *The Fullness of the Spirit,* Kansas City, Nazarene Publishing House, *1958*

Hayford, Jack W, *Worship His Majesty,* Waco, TX, Word Books, 1987

Lea, Larry, *Could You Not Tarry One Hour, Charisma House, 1985*

MacMillan, John, *The Authority of the Believer,* Christian Publishers, 1981

McIntosh & Martin, *Finding Them, Keeping Them, B&H Books, 1991*

Murray, Andrew, *Humility,* Whitaker House, 1982

Nee, Watchman, *Spiritual Authority,* Christian Fellowship Publishers, New York, 1972

Wimber, John, *Power Healing, HarperOne, Reprint Edition, 2009*

Ruth, C.W, *Entire Sanctification Explained,* Kansas City, Beacon Hill Press, 1952

Seamands, David, *Healing for Damaged Emotions, David C. Cook, 1992*

Slocum, Robert E., *Maximize Your Ministry* ,Colorado Springs, NavPress, 1990

Strait, C. Neil, *To be Holy: Principles for living the Spirit* , Kansas City, Beacon Hill Press, 1984

Taylor, Willard H, "Ephesians," A.F. Harper, ed., *Beacon Bible Commentary, Volume 9,* Kansas City, Beacon Hill Press, 1965

Wood, A. Skevington, "Ephesians," Frank E. Gaebelein, ed., *The Expositor's Bible Commentary, Volume 11,* Grand Rapids, Zondervan Publishing House,1978

Wagner, C. Peter, *How to Grow a Church,* Ventura, CA, Regal Books, 1976

Wagner, C. Peter, *The Third Wave of the Holy Spirit: Encountering the Power of Signs and Wonders Today,* Vine Books, 1988

Warner, Timothy M., *Spiritual Warfare, Victory over the Powers of This Dark World,* Wheaton, IL, Crossway Books, 1991

Webster's New World Dictionary, The World Publishing Company, 1958,59

www.ingramcontent.com/pod-product-compliance
Lightning Source LLC
Chambersburg PA
CBHW081512040426
42447CB00013B/3199